HEARING THE VOICE OF GOD

ALEX AND HANNAH ABSALOM

Dandelion Resourcing
dandelionresourcing.com

Hearing the Voice of God

- Biblical and practical ways to hear the voice of Jesus and step into the gift of prophecy

Copyright © 2019 Alex and Hannah Absalom

Published by Dandelion Resourcing - dandelionresourcing.com

While all the stories in this book are true, some names and identifying information have been changed for the sake of privacy.

To contact the authors about speaking at your conference or church, please go to dandelionresourcing.com.

Design and Layout: Caity Shinnick

ISBN: 978-1-951420-00-0 (paperback)

ISBN: 978-1-951420-01-7 (ebook)

Library of Congress Control Number: 2019913057

1. Gifts, Spiritual. 2. Prophecy–Christianity. 234.13

CONTENTS

INTRODUCTION

Welcome To The Naturally Supernatural Series!

We are a family of missionaries - Mum, Dad, and three sons - who in 2007 were called to move from England to the United States, back when our boys were small and Alex had more hair!

Having now lived in three very different parts of the country, we can say that we love this calling! We have had the privilege of speaking to tens of thousands of Christians, coaching many hundreds of leaders, consulting with dozens of churches and denominations, as well as always being fully involved in local church leadership - ranging from megachurches to church planting.

During this time, it has been exciting to see the wider church in the US develop a stronger emphasis upon discipleship, particularly a drive towards creating cultures that intentionally form disciple-making disciples of Jesus. There is a deeper recognition that discipleship must be built around life imitation, rather than simply reducing it to information transfer.

Likewise, we have also observed an increased focus on equipping believers to go with the Gospel. More people are being actively encouraged to carry the words and works of Jesus into their neighborhoods, communities, workplaces, and schools. While great Sunday morning church services are wonderful, growing numbers of leaders are realizing that simultaneously we must also encourage new expressions of church to form throughout the week, wherever the lost are already gathering and can be discipled.

THE MISSING PIECE

Yet there is still a piece missing alongside disciple-making and living on mission, which for us is summed up by the phrase 'naturally supernatural'. **As disciples of Jesus, we need to be people who operate in the power and the authority of the Holy Spirit.**

Sometimes this will mean opening our mouths and sharing the Good News of the Gospel. Other times it will be modeling the servant leadership that Jesus calls us to embody. And on other occasions we will make use of the gifts of the Spirit, bringing healing, deliverance, prophecies, faith, and the like as part of the expansion of God's heavenly Kingdom here on earth.

In all of these things, we will be empowered to exhibit the fruit of the Spirit to all who encounter us, because if we do not have love, we are nothing (1 Corinthians 13:2-3).

To be naturally supernatural means that we demonstrate these more supernatural marks of the Spirit's empowering throughout our lives - to the extent that it simply seems natural and normal to anyone observing. And while we know that these things can only come from God's Spirit, at the same time they should be normal and normative, rather than strange and random.

One of our surprises living in the US has been the apathy in many Christians towards this life in the Spirit, particularly to the more seemingly supernatural gifts. (Of course, every spiritual gift requires the anointing of the Spirit to do well, but we recognize that there are some that are genuinely impossible for us to produce simply by our hard work.)

Perhaps it is the relative ease of calling yourself a Christian in the United States when compared to most other Western nations, let alone the rest of the world. If deciding to follow Christ proves to be a culturally comfortable choice, then it makes sense that many will not feel a daily need to press into the Spirit's authority and continual empowering.

In some cases this is due to open hostility towards the gifts being active today. Cessationism (the belief that the gifts of the Spirit died out once the Bible was written) has had an especially warm reception amongst some American denominations. It is a classic example of a theology being built in an attempt to justify an experience (in this case, a lack of supernatural activity), which tragically has resulted in countless Christians being taught that the gifts of the Spirit 'are not for today'. (Of course, the same challenge is likewise there for those whose worldview does allow for naturally supernatural ministry: we must first start from Scripture, and then allow that to interpret experience, rather than the other way around.)

For others, the issue is not so much theological as practical - just **how do we operate in these things while remaining a people deeply shaped by Scripture?** And where can we find clear and wise practices to learn from? This is the imitation paradox: many people we speak with have never seen naturally supernatural living modeled in ways that are accessible and desirable, and so, in turn, they don't know how to model it to those they lead.

OUR BACKGROUNDS: EVANGELICAL AND NATURALLY SUPERNATURAL

Of course, there are some wonderful churches and ministries who beautifully model naturally supernatural living. We have been fortunate to experience a number of such communities, and have benefitted from their stories, experiences, and teachings. However, many who come from evangelical backgrounds often don't feel comfortable in such environments, and much is lost in translation between the two tribes.

Our own stories of encountering life in the Spirit (which we tell in greater depth in our book *Being Filled with the Holy Spirit*, which is part of this series) have always been rooted in a strong evangelical theology. The centrality of the cross of Christ and His atoning work there, belief in the literal resurrection, a high view of Scripture, the urgency of sharing the Good News of Jesus, and an understanding that following Jesus has to be lived out in the world, are foundational planks of our faith.

To pursue the present day activity of the Holy Spirit through the gifts of the Spirit requires zero diminishment of those core beliefs. We would argue that **a naturally supernatural lifestyle is one that is far more faithful to the clear commands of Christ**, the example of the early church in Acts, and the teachings of Paul. It is actually MORE honoring to the Bible to be naturally supernatural in your beliefs and practice!

We have been in full-time church leadership since 1994, and throughout we have pursued both a deeper commitment to Scripture and a simultaneous deepening of our experience of the Spirit's empowering. One feeds the other, and thus we are drawn closer to Christ and, hopefully, to greater conformity to Him.

WHY THIS SERIES

Over recent years we have found ourselves teaching more and more on living a naturally supernatural lifestyle, both at conferences and with individuals and small groups. Friends began to encourage us to write on this area, but, to be honest, we didn't want to do so unless Jesus really made this clear to us.

One day, as Alex was spending time with the Lord, he unexpectedly saw a clear vision of a series of shorter books that tackled different topics, all under the banner of 'Naturally Supernatural'. The mandate was to produce something that would equip the church, combining strong Scriptural teaching with field-tested practical 'how-tos' for implementation, mixed in with stories, activation exercises, study guides, passages to memorize, Q&As, prayers, and anything that would help individuals, groups, and churches to step into these areas with these books as field guides. For us, this book series does indeed feel like a call from God.

Topics we cover in the series include the prophetic gifts, healing, deliverance, building a Kingdom theology, being filled with the Holy Spirit, tongues, miracles, faith, and becoming a naturally supernatural missionary.

WHY THIS BOOK

This is the first book in the series because **the ability to hear God's voice is foundational to everything else that is part of the naturally supernatural life**. Indeed, as you will see, we believe that knowing how to hear and respond in faith to what Jesus is saying is actually the very basis of what it means to be a disciple.

You will learn what it means to prophesy (which is the Biblical term for hearing and appropriately sharing what you sense the Lord might be saying to you), and then we will break prophecy down into the three main constituent parts: revelation, interpretation, and application. Along the way we will share practical tips, give you shareable trainings, and reveal pitfalls to avoid - so that you can step into the prophetic in ways that are healthy and life-giving to others.

You will see that the book is divided into two sections: core teaching and next steps. Our desire is to give you a clear grounding in Scriptural principles and practical teaching on hearing God's voice, into which are added a wide variety of ways for you to step into the gift of prophecy, which are designed to suit different personalities and spiritualities. Have fun playing with these (yes, you can have fun when experimenting with becoming more naturally supernatural!), and allow Jesus to show you where you can grow and develop further.

The goal throughout is to help you take specific, tangible next steps, and then to be able to help other people do likewise. This will mean taking risks - but it is a lifestyle that Jesus commends!

"Therefore everyone who hears these words of mine and puts them into practice is like a wise man who built his house on the rock."
Matthew 7:24

PART I

CORE TEACHING

The first part of this book is focused on providing you with teaching and content. This will give you a strong foundation from the Scriptures for hearing God's voice, along with proven practical training that equips you in the actual mechanics of how to do this in bold yet wise ways.

However, be warned - even at this early stage we will focus unashamedly on your next steps, so putting this into practice is woven throughout!

This section will come to you in 6 chapters:

1. Our Hearing Problem - Explaining why we have such a strong need to hear God's voice, and how to overcome any negative perceptions and experiences of the prophetic that might be in play.

2. Defining Prophecy - Here you will gain a clear understanding of what prophecy is (and isn't!), including common characteristics. You will also see how it is presented throughout the New Testament.

3. Revelation - A description of 12 different ways that God might speak to you today, including clear explanations of what it 'feels' like when He does so. This will enable you, and those you train, to better recognize God's voice in the moment.

4. How to Share Revelation - Some coaching on if, when and how to share a prophecy, and how to do so with a wisdom and sensitivity that builds up the recipient(s). This is vital to prevent misuse of this powerful gift.

5. Interpretation - We all need to know how to weigh or test a prophetic word, and in this chapter you learn 6 principles for doing just that.

6. Application - Here you are given 10 different steps for applying a prophecy, so that you, or those you are training, can have a clear process for knowing what to do with prophetic revelation.

1

OUR HEARING PROBLEM

S oon after establishing his Ear, Nose and Throat (ENT) medical practice in 1950s France, Alfred Tomatis unexpectedly found himself treating singers referred to him by his professional opera singer father.

The performers came seeking help because they had mysteriously lost the ability to hit certain notes that they knew were within their vocal range. It was as if some notes were being bypassed - which made no sense to the performers, or to other doctors they'd consulted, who incorrectly thought it was a physical problem to do with the vocal cords.

But Dr Tomatis had a hunch it was something else - less about the voice, and more about hearing. So he decided to run an experiment on his theory by setting up a sonometer to measure the noise level of those opera singers in full song. He found that from 1 meter an opera star produced 140 decibels of sound - louder than an emergency siren, and the same as a jet engine at take off. And if that was the volume measured externally, he knew that it would be even louder inside the singer's skull.

Tomatis thus proposed that the opera stars didn't have a voice problem, but a hearing one. They were literally deafening themselves by the very loudness of their own singing! More specifically, their voices had damaged the muscles of their inner ear - meaning that they could no longer hear certain notes that they were meant to be singing.

Put another way, their ability to listen had been completely disrupted. He postulated a theory: if you can't hear a note, then you can't sing it.

YOU ARE DESIGNED TO HEAR!

As followers of Jesus who are eager to hear His voice in every situation of life, we can learn a lot from the story of Dr. Tomatis and his research.

Wherever we are on our spiritual journey,

God loves to speak to us far more than we realize.

When Jesus died on the cross, it was to bring us back into a full and complete relationship with God our loving Father. And like any healthy relationship, the ability to hear one another clearly is essential.

God's heart for you is that you know Him so personally! It's all about this relationship – we are children with our loving Father. Thus Paul wrote in Ephesians 1:17, *"I keep asking that the God of our Lord Jesus Christ, the glorious Father, may give you the Spirit of wisdom and revelation, so that you may know him better."*

When Jesus declared that *"My sheep know my voice"* (John 10:27), He was telling us that we are designed for a familiarity with God that is both reverent and intimate, where there'll be moments of such intertwining that we'll look back and not be sure whether it was His voice or our decision that led us forward.

This book is all about hearing God's voice - the Biblical foundations, the practical realities, the mechanics, and the safeguards. It is designed to bring healing to damaged hearing, and confidence that we can indeed recognize and respond to the voice of the Creator of the universe.

However, before we dive into the nature of prophecy, and how we can see it develop in our lives, we need to first pull down false thinking and self-defeating behaviors when it comes to hearing God.

DROWNING OUT GOD'S VOICE

The sheer number of competing voices to which we give our attention mean that, like Dr Tomatis' opera singing patients, we often end up deafening ourselves to God's call. Whether it is our own negative self-talk, the critical chatter of others, the voice of condemnation from the enemy, or simply the constant noise of our culture, all of them combine to incrementally diminish our attentiveness to God's words.

As followers of Jesus, our spiritual journey is one that experiences highs and lows, successes and failures, breakthroughs and problems. Probably like you, my own tendency in the tricky times is to wish, "If only my voice could be heard more clearly and loudly", believing that what I have is a speech problem.

However, the painful reality is that, both in the valley and on the mountain top, the far greater issue is that I have a listening problem. Because I'm just not very good at listening to the voice of God.

One way Christians justify this inattention is to come up with flaky theologies built on the unbiblical idea that God is a Father who doesn't much like to personally chat with His children, except perhaps to chastise us when we step too far out of line. "We have the eternal truths of Scripture to guide us" we affirm, mistakenly creating a false either-or narrative, which pits welcoming the prophetic gifts against being a people deeply formed by the Bible. But it is not an either-or, but a both-and, which God, our very communicative Father, wants for us.

Ironically, though, even when we turn to Scripture, we still often miss what Jesus is saying to us in our specific time and place.

We fill our lives with so much noise that we drown out God's beating heart over us.

The moment we awake, most of us reach immediately for our phones where social media and limitless news articles greet us. My phone brazenly greets me with this perfectly designed distraction list. "Alex - here are your top stories." "Wow," I think, "curated stories, just for me? Awesome! I am SO special!" I'd happily read and watch them for hours, filling every moment with those things.

The price of all that clutter is that we stop prayer-dreaming. We quench the creative spark of our God who is the source of all wisdom and answers, if only we could pause to ask, rest, listen and obey.

By cranking up the volume on the noise, we have diminished our ability to hear God's voice, and thus our ability to respond in faith. The extraneous fluff of our culture provides us with a different rhythm to dance to, which we find ourselves often unable to resist.

REDISCOVERING GOD'S TIMBRE

Timbre is a word that describes the distinctive properties of a sound. It is the characteristics of a voice (or instrument), and is what lets you distinguish one voice from another.

God's voice has a unique heavenly timbre.

It carries a resonant and distinctive tone, which is bubbling over with love, hope and majesty. It is essential to the fullness of life that Jesus offers that we learn how to tune ourselves into His voice more firmly than all of the other options.

Without this understanding, we find ourselves crushed, worn down, and adrift.

- When your friend who is addicted feels utterly condemned and thinks that's from Jesus, they have lost track of the sound of Jesus, the one who brings conviction and hope, but never condemnation (Romans 8:1).

- When your colleague with a broken marriage feels abandoned and alone, they have lost that pulsating

Kingdom rhythm that tells them, *"I will never leave you nor forsake you"* (Hebrews 13:5).

- When your sister says that she is worn out by juggling sick kids, a mean boss, and not enough cash, she needs to experience in her heart of hearts the voice of Jesus offering her true rest (Matthew 11:28-30).

We live today with lives that are so loud, and schedules that are so busy, that we find it really tough to tune into what Jesus is saying in the everyday moments of life. Both literally and metaphorically, there is background noise everywhere.

At night time, Hannah and I like to sleep with the bedroom window open, but as we live in the city there is constant noise around our home. The intrusion of 2am fire trucks and slamming doors and yelling drunk people propelled Hannah to start using a sound machine at night - which seems crazy: we make more noise to blot out the noise!

Gordon Hempton is something called an audio ecologist. He has devoted his life to finding places devoid of human sound - which he defines as 15 minutes uninterrupted quiet in daylight hours. He has produced a list of the last great quiet places, and currently it shows that only 12 places in the whole of the continental USA meet his criteria. It is astounding that even with the Rockies and the Great Plains, so few places (and people) experience uninterrupted quiet.

Down the ages, Christians have found that God tends to speak the clearest when we are the quietest. But when it comes to God, we deafen ourselves to hearing Him, because we are constantly making or surrounded by noise. I heard someone say recently that **"quiet is the think tank of the soul."** Psalm 46:1 begins with a very similar sentiment: *"Be still and know that I am God."*

Quiet is so important because usually God speaks in a quiet voice. "Why would God do that?" we ask, noisily. I wonder if the reason is that the person listening has to lean in to hear properly — and...

> *The goal of hearing the voice of God is not hearing the voice of God, but intimacy with our Father.*

When our three sons were small, they could make an incredible amount of noise charging around inside on wet English winter (and summer!) days. So they heard many times our declaration, "Indoor voices, boys!" (as we tried to deliver said message without using our outdoor voices). God, of course, has a jolly loud outdoor voice, with which He could easily blast us. Fortunately, though, it is usually His indoor voice that He uses. And so we lean in, and find ourselves unexpectedly experiencing afresh His heart of love for us and for those to whom He has sent us as His representatives.

Which is where prophecy comes in. As Kris Vallotton puts it, "Prophecy, in its simplest form, is merely hearing from the Holy Spirit and repeating what He said." Moses prayed in Numbers 11:29:

> *"Would that all the Lord's people were prophets, that the Lord would put His Spirit upon them!"*

This is what Christ has done for us, and is a wonderful gift in drawing us closer to our Heavenly Father's wild and wonderful love.

MENDING DAMAGED HEARING

Let's go back to our struggling opera singers. Dr Tomatis obviously wasn't satisfied with diagnosing their hearing loss, as he wanted to help them rediscover what had been damaged and lost. After a lot of research, he found that you can retrain the muscles of the inner ear so that it can function again without distortion.

Tomatis developed three core theories about the function of the ear.

1. Its initial purpose is to grow the brain of the unborn child, as it is the first sense to be developed when the fetus is only a few months old. Stories abound of how a fetus can learn and recognize sounds within the womb, and how as a newborn she can hear her mother's voice and be immediately comforted.

We unwittingly devised our own experiment with our eldest son Joel. Throughout the pregnancy we devotedly watched a daily TV show with a very distinctive and melodic theme tune ('Neighbours', for British and Australian readers!) - and as a tiny newborn, the music would come on and he would stop crying!

2. After birth the ear's role is to re-energize the neocortex of the brain, which is the area where the central nervous system is located. If there is a malfunction of the ear, the nervous system inhibits our ability to take on board information, communicate clearly, and have healthy social interactions.

3. The ear has a huge impact on our voices, as heard sounds are tested and repeated by the emerging vocal set-up. Although some other specialists disagree, Tomatis believed that the voice can only produce what the ear can hear.

Leaving aside any medical debate about the details of Tomatis' theories, we can take these three theories and apply them spiritually to our ability to hear the voice of God.

1. Our first need is to be able to hear God's voice. It is foundational to our development, and also to a deep sense of comfort that we are also meant to carry through life. To grow as disciple-making disciples of Jesus, the first sense we should develop is spiritual hearing.

2. We need a healthy ability to hear God's voice in order to take on spiritual truths and wisdom. This in turn becomes the staging post for us to grow further towards maturity in Christ. Even with the Bible open in front of us, we are reliant upon the Holy Spirit to make sense of what it is that we are reading. This applies even more so as we go out into the world and seek to act as Christ's ambassadors, who can represent Jesus and His Kingdom through our words, values and deeds.

3. If we desire to be a voice that honors God by the way we bless and develop others, we need to be deeply attuned to the voice of the Father. Jesus said, *"For I did not speak on my own, but the Father who sent me commanded me to say all that I have spoken."* (John 12:49). This means that anyone can speak out the Father's heart (prophecy), so long as they can tune their ear to the voice of God. (Incidentally, is not the same thing as being spiritually mature - you can have accurate prophetic words given by immature people.)

So whether you need a complete introduction to the sound of God's voice, training in how to easily spot and lock onto His timbre, or simply some fine tuning in developing these skills further, this book is designed to equip you, as well as those you lead and disciple.

GRACE FOR THE HARD OF HEARING

As you think about the ability to hear God's voice, it might be that you look at others who seem to hear Him so clearly and feel a personal sense of discouragement. "She clicks with Jesus so readily - whereas I'm still here wondering if that little thought that flitted through my mind is because the room is too warm, I ate a lot of cheese at dinner, or if somehow it might be God!"

If you are a Christian, then we guarantee that you do hear God's voice!

For a start, it's impossible to be saved without the Father taking the initiative to call you to Himself, an effort to which you then responded. And Jesus has continued to nudge and prompt and stir you in all sorts of times and places since then, and you will have responded in admirable ways to many of those moments.

However, the comparison game is never going to produce healthy outcomes. There is always going to be someone who 'gets it' more than we do, and seems to hear God more clearly. Yet we believe that...

What God looks for most is not the ability to hear, but the heart to hear Him

Think of a parent with a child. When they are in a noisy room with hundreds of others talking, the parent doesn't become cross if the child can't hear them quietly call their name, because they realize the circumstances require them to take the initiative to raise their voice. In a moment of danger - imagine the child is about to run out into the street after a runaway ball - the volume of the parental voice will go straight up to full blast, as all intervening levels are bypassed! Yet later that day, when the parent sits on the edge of the child's bed to wake them after a nap, they will do so with a gentle whisper.

Likewise, our Heavenly Father understands each one of us so well, and adjusts His approach and expectations according to who and where we are. If our hearts are humble and we hunger to hear His voice more clearly, then we will not be condemned if we don't catch every word. He knows **it is a journey of us learning how to hear again**, and that in this fallen world we will never get it right 100% of the time.

So, please give yourself grace. Don't focus on what others hear (or don't hear), and instead put your attention upon the Lover of your soul. Simply be hungry for more of Him, and you will steadily increase in your ability and confidence to hear God's voice.

———

Hannah's Story

I (Hannah) would like to take a moment and share a little bit of my journey in terms of hearing God's voice. I grew up in a home and a church (in the UK) which believed in, welcomed and practiced the gifts of the Spirit. From time to time I had experiences of hearing God speak, which left me in no doubt that He was real and working in and through me.

However, this way of operating was not a lifestyle, but a few one-off events. When Alex and I met and started praying together, I quickly realized that he was way more gifted than me and would hear God's voice all the time. This was very frustrating for me, as he was the newer Christian, and so at times I felt like just giving up! Frequently we'd pray together and he would ask me if I felt God say anything, and I would just answer, "No!"

Alex encouraged me to keep persevering, and I intentionally made that choice. Now, after several decades of hungering for more of the Spirit and specifically asking for the gift of prophecy, I have grown tremendously. While the prophetic is not my number one area of gifting, through lots of practice and much stepping out in faith, it is an area in which I can very competently operate. I see a lot of fruit both in my life and through me in others' lives - which, of course, is both exciting and encouraging.

Sometimes hearing God's voice is easy and just happens, sometimes it takes a lot of hunger and pressing in over a period of time, but it is our strong belief that **God is speaking and will continue to speak to and through every believer**.

Prayer Exercise

Before we jump into more content, here is a preparatory prayer exercise to help set your heart in the right place as you seek to grow in hearing God's voice.

1. Location

Find a quiet place where you can sit comfortably and undisturbed for 5 - 10 minutes.

2. Gratitude for Access

As you settle down, begin by thanking Jesus for making it possible for you to come straight into the Father's presence. *"We have confidence to enter the Most Holy Place by the blood of Jesus."* (Hebrews 10:19)

3. Scripture

Slowly read out loud each of these verses. With each one, repeat the verse a second time, but personalize it to you, e.g. "I call on You Father, and I know that You will answer me, and tell me great and unsearchable things that I have not known."

- *"I will instruct you and teach you in the way you should go; I will counsel you with my loving eye on you. Do not be like the horse or the mule, which have no understanding but must be controlled by bit and bridle or they will not come to you."* (Psalm 32:8-9)

- *"Call to me and I will answer you and tell you great and unsearchable things you do not know."* (Jeremiah 33:3)

- *"My sheep listen to my voice; I know them, and they follow me."* (John 10:27)

- *"So faith comes from hearing, and hearing through the word of Christ."* (Romans 10:17 ESV)

- *"Whoever has ears, let them hear what the Spirit says to the churches."* (Revelation 3:22)

4. End by:

- Declaring that it is foundational to hear God's voice.

- Committing yourself to this as an ever-developing pattern for your life.

- Asking Jesus to answer this prayer in ways beyond your imagination or experience up to now!

DEFINING PROPHECY

There is so much confusion about the prophetic gifts, so let's begin by creating a clear definition. Further on in this chapter we'll share some language that others use, but, for now, here is what we mean:

> *Prophecy is the loving supernatural ability to know and appropriately speak the mind of God on a specific subject at a specific time by the prompting and inspiration of the Holy Spirit.*

A few things to note:

- Prophecy is a **supernatural** ability - it comes from God and is to glorify God, through both the process (how we prophesy) and the outcome (what we prophesy).

- It is rooted and grounded in **love. To share accurate prophetic words without love is to miss the point entirely.**

- When we talk about knowing the **mind of God**, this is

not a universal statement - no human could possibly know more than a droplet of what God knows! Yet **we can have the mind of Christ - God's insight, wisdom, and understanding - on a specific matter**. Paul wrote about this in 1 Corinthians 2. His focus in that chapter is on ensuring that the church's faith is not built upon human wisdom, but divine power (v.5). He states clearly that part of our task is to declare and demonstrate God's wisdom - which quite clearly we can't do out of our own cleverness, skills or strength.

- The way we are to access that divine wisdom is **through the Holy Spirit** revealing these things to us. As Paul wrote in v.11, *"For who knows a person's thoughts except their own spirit within them? In the same way no one knows the thoughts of God except the Spirit of God."* Christian prophecy is something that is only possible when it is prompted and inspired by the Holy Spirit.

- This expression of the wisdom of God in prophecy **is specific** rather than universal. It is for a specific person or community in a specific place at a specific point in time. This is one of the ways that it is different from, and inferior to, Scripture. The Bible is God's wisdom revealed by the Spirit to all people in all places at all times. So to believe in the use of the prophetic gifts in no way undermines our high value on the Bible. In fact, done right, it only builds our value for Scripture since, as we'll discover, the Bible is not only the primary way God speaks to us, but is also our first benchmark for evaluating a prophecy.

KEY TEXTS

1 Corinthians 14:1 and 3 are critical texts for creating a framework for our pursuit of prophecy.

"Follow the way of love and eagerly desire gifts of the Spirit, especially prophecy… the one who prophesies speaks to people for their strengthening, encouraging and comfort."

Out of those verses, and allied with some nearby passages, we can draw some more foundational insights about the nature of prophecy.

1. PROPHECY IS ALL ABOUT LOVE

In 1 Corinthians 13:2, Paul writes: *"If I have the gift of prophecy and can fathom all mysteries and all knowledge… but do not have love, I am nothing."*

The point of prophecy is that it is all about love - meaning the thing that is patient, kind, not envious, not proud, and so on!

The enemy tries to bring guilt, shame, and condemnation, but we should bring love.

This doesn't mean that prophecy can't challenge or provoke us to repentance and change (it often does!), but it must always come from a heart of love in us (if we are sharing), and reveal the Father's heart of love for that person or community (so the receiver is aware of that love).

Galatians 5:6 tells us that *"The only thing that counts is faith expressing itself through love."* Often people feel anxiety about prophecy, particularly where it seems strange or spooky. We can help calm that by a tone that is kind and grace-filled, ensuring that what we share reveals God's loving Father heart.

Interestingly, Paul tells us (1 Corinthians 14:1) that we follow the way of love when we *"eagerly desire"* the gifts of the Holy Spirit. The English term 'gifts of the Holy Spirit' in the original Greek is actually something much simpler - literally, 'the spiritual'. English translations add the word 'gifts' to help unpack the meaning. But in essence, Paul tells us to 'eagerly desire the spiritual stuff'!

According to Paul, we perhaps most follow the way of love when we prophesy. Now that is a ministry-changing insight!

Shawn Bolz comments on why Paul so highlights prophecy out of all the gifts: "It can be one of the clearest validations of the Father's great love, which Jesus paid such a high price for. When people hear the thoughts and emotions of God toward them, they believe in his love for them."

2. Prophecy Connects Us with God

The point of prophecy is to connect us to the Father. Paul writes, *"I keep asking that the God of our Lord Jesus Christ, the glorious Father, may give you the Spirit of wisdom and revelation, so that you may know him better"* (Ephesians 1:17).

It is easy to miss what is going on here. Paul is not asking for us to grow in gifts of wisdom and revelation (good though that is). Instead, the prayer is for us to experience more of

God's Spirit of revelation and wisdom, so that we can know the Father better.

Insights into the character, heart, and mind of God can only come by the anointing of the Holy Spirit. And the goal of revelation from God is that we, or others with whom we share revelation, may know the Father more deeply.

Bear in mind that in the biblical understanding, knowledge of God is never in the abstract - it is always tied to obedience and intimacy. If you don't do what He says, you don't know Him, however much information about Him might be in your head.

Although prophecy brings some beautiful and profound insights into our lives, ultimately that is not its purpose. The point is to know and love God, as the Holy Spirit reveals more about the Father to us and through us, to His great glory.

3. PROPHECY IS OPEN TO ALL

Prophecy is something that anyone who is committed to Christ can do. While we won't all have the same level of clarity, regularity, or insight, nevertheless the prophetic gifts (by which we mean prophecy, words of knowledge, words of wisdom, distinguishing between spirits) are open to ALL of us!

Think of it like this: it would be so cruel and deceptive of Paul to urge us all to *"eagerly desire gifts of the Spirit, especially prophecy"* if lots of us were automatically excluded from accessing them! Clearly he isn't doing that - and thus we conclude from Scripture (as well as from experience) that **anyone who loves the Lord Jesus can learn to prophesy**.

Paul's instruction to eagerly desire to prophesy flows directly out of Chapter 13's masterpiece on love. If we view the love passage as being mandatory for all followers of Jesus, by what strange twist of exposition does the start of Chapter 14 on prophecy abruptly stop being for everyone? Paul deeply ties the pursuit of love to the pursuit of the gifts of the Spirit.

> *Eagerly desiring the gifts is an invitation to everyone who follows Jesus.*

4. PROPHECY IS A CHOICE

To eagerly desire means that we CHOOSE to learn, practice, and intentionally grow in our skills in this area. It is a partnership between us and the Spirit.

Candidly, we have met many people who simply don't want to access these gifts! That might seem extraordinary to you, but it is far more common in some church circles than you imagine.

* PAUSE and consider: on a scale of 1 to 5, how eagerly do you desire that you might prophesy?

5. PROPHECY IS TO STRENGTHEN, ENCOURAGE AND COMFORT

Prophecy is for *"strengthening, encouraging and comfort."* This is our non-negotiable ground rule for anyone starting out and becoming established in the prophetic gifts.

And it is such an invitation! After all, wouldn't you like to be more strengthening, encouraging and comforting to others? Wouldn't you like it, when you're helping, advising, and leading others, for it to be less about your own wise words and instead for God to speak through you right into the heart of the situation? Wouldn't you like a reduction of the pressure on you to come up with something 'good' to say? This is a gift to both the hearer and to the sharer!

Kris Vallotton says, "True prophetic ministry looks for the gold in the midst of the dirt of people's lives." In other words, there are no prizes for spotting the junk and the dysfunction. Instead, if we start with how the Father sees them, who He wants them to become, isn't that spirit of encouragement far more likely to bring out the sort of sincere repentance and profound life change that is characteristic of encountering Jesus?

6. Prophecy can be Hindsight, Insight or Foresight

Prophecy itself works in three time frames. It can be **hindsight about what we already know, insight into the present, or foresight into the future**.

- **Hindsight** is generally either to gain our attention (often this is called a Word of Knowledge), or to help us look back with better understanding, discernment, and wisdom.

- **Insight** is to help us make sense of what is going on around us, and in particular what the Father is saying and doing, so that we can follow His lead more closely.

- **Foresight** tells us what could be if we partner with the Lord, and thus is often focused on our preparation. Sometimes it tells us about things that God has in mind to bring about.

7. PROPHECY HELPS FORM DISCIPLE-MAKING DISCIPLES

Prophecy is closely tied to being a disciple of Jesus. If you recall, Jesus is at pains to point out that being a disciple means that we hear and obey what He is saying (e.g. Luke 6:46-49). In the New Testament…

Discipleship is always obedience-based.

However, in order to obey we must know what Jesus is saying specifically about our personal context. While some situations are fully covered by God's universal principles (e.g. 'Can I pocket this pile of cash that is sitting on my colleagues' desk?'), that is not always the case.

What about those times when we're wanting to follow biblical principles, but there are several valid options for the situation at hand? For example, do you follow the advice of Psalm 27:14 and *"Wait patiently for the Lord…"*, or do you instead go with Philippians 3:12 and *"…press on to take hold of that for which Christ Jesus took hold of me?"*

We each have times where we are trying to discern between more nuanced options, all of which might be morally good, but yet will lead us down very divergent paths (e.g. Should I take this new job? What school should our child go to? Is it wise to take out a loan to do this additional training?)

These are the bread and butter issues of applied discipleship. And it is in these circumstances that we want to hear if Jesus is saying something specific to us. Sometimes this is by us hearing God's voice for ourselves, and sometimes it is through prophetic words from others. And, of course, sometimes we will be that external prophetic voice for those around us.

There are plenty of times where Jesus is perfectly happy for us to demonstrate maturity and make the choice ourselves. After all, He is seeking to build a family full of sons and daughters, not a factory full of slaves. However, we all recognize that there are also times where we definitely need His leading, or where He wants to more overtly steer us.

Yet how can we follow and learn from Jesus if we don't know how to hear His voice? This is why this is such a vital skill!

8. Prophecy Comes as Revelation, Interpretation and Application

We have found that generally **a prophetic word has three parts — revelation, interpretation, and application**.

- **Revelation** is about what Jesus is actually saying to us, and the mechanics of how He does that.

- **Interpretation** is about weighing what has been sensed, and discerning if and how much of it is from Jesus, and what it might mean to us today.

- **Application** is about deciding what I am going to do in response. Will I respond in faith and obedience? What is the timeline? What are my next steps?

Much of the rest of this book unpacks those three headings - each will have its own chapter.

SOME OTHER DEFINITIONS

Here is how some others have defined prophecy:

- Ben Witherington: "Prophecy is not a sermon by C21 standards. It is a spontaneous utterance prompted by the Spirit and based upon a sudden, uncontrolled revelation from God."

- Peter Wagner: "The gift of prophecy is the special ability that God gives to members of the Body of Christ to receive and communicate an immediate message of God to his gathered people, a group among them or any one of his people individually, through a divinely anointed utterance."

- Greg Haslam: "Prophecy is a phenomenon that results directly from the access God has to our minds, whereby He can create pictures in our imagination, give supernatural dreams while we sleep, and put words and ideas out of Scripture into our heads with such a force that we know there is something weighty and unforgettable going on, something that carries with it the responsibility to pass on and relay what the Holy Spirit has communicated."

- Shawn Bolz: "The goal of revelation is so simple: See what God sees, hear what God hears, and speak what God speaks so we can all love the way God loves.

Revelation is given to us so we can carry a piece of God's heart from eternity into the world."

- Mike Bickle: "We prophesy each time we make known His passionate heart."

PROPHETIC EXAMPLES FROM THE NEW TESTAMENT

In order to continue to anchor your understanding of and confidence in the prophetic gifts, here are some examples from the New Testament of prophetic gifts in action.

THE EXAMPLE OF JESUS

Jesus is incredibly prophetic throughout His ministry on earth. Leaving aside that His birth, life, death and resurrection fulfill over 320 Old Testament prophecies, He Himself exercises prophetic gifts on many occasions. For instance:

- He 'knows' that the woman at the well has had many husbands, and that she's not married to her current man (John 4:17-18). But Jesus doesn't say this to hurt or shame her, but rather to express His love and compassion to her, and draw her closer to Him. (Bear in mind that in the culture of the time, a husband could toss aside a wife for the slightest offense - like burning his dinner - simply by declaring out loud three times, 'I divorce you'. Our modern eyes read this as a condemnation of a commitment-shy and morally loose woman, whereas maybe Jesus saw a wounded woman who had been treated with repeated unkindness and lack of love by many men.)

- Jesus predicts Peter's denial (Luke 22:34)

- He 'sees' Nathaniel under the tree before they meet, which Nathaniel clearly interprets as a prophetic word (John 1:48)

- Jesus foretells the destruction of Jerusalem (Mark 13)

- Jesus summarizes the essence of His ministry when He states in John 5:19, *"The Son can do nothing by himself; he can do only what he sees his Father doing, because whatever the Father does the Son also does."* He shared this not to brag about His divinity, but to give us a model to aim for in how we live our lives and make our choices in orientation to our loving Heavenly Father.

THE EXAMPLE OF THE EARLY CHURCH

The Acts of the Apostles - a book which could far more accurately be titled 'The Acts of the Holy Spirit' - is packed full of prophetic people, actions and insights.

- When Peter is filled with the Spirit at Pentecost and preaches under that same anointing, he turns to Joel 2 as an interpretative key to understand all the things that are happening around them. Peter (and the early church) are clear: the Holy Spirit is poured out upon believers in Christ, the 'last days' have begun, and one of the key signs - Peter labors the point - is that God's servants, both male and female, will prophesy (Acts 2:17-18).

- In Acts 5:3 Peter knew by the Spirit that Ananias, and later Sapphira, were lying.

- In Acts 8:29 the Spirit told Philip, *"Go to that chariot and stay near it."* That simple prophetic word led to the conversion and baptism of the Ethiopian eunuch, and the resulting planting of the church in East Africa.

- Agabus prophesies about a coming famine (Acts 11:28), and later he foretells Paul's arrest and imprisonment in Jerusalem (Acts 21:11). Judging by the way he is described, he was a man who clearly had a pattern of sharing accurate prophetic words.

- In Acts 14:9 we read that the lame man *"listened to Paul as he was speaking. Paul looked directly at him, saw that he had faith to be healed"*, to which comes the obvious question, just how do you 'see' faith? Clearly this was a prophetic revelation from the Spirit (and a good example of one of the ways that prophetic revelation comes, when people just 'know' stuff.)

- In Acts 21:9 we read that Philip *"had four unmarried daughters who prophesied"*. Luke was obviously struck by this family - and wished to hold it out not as an exception but a norm that all parents can strive for. We should be raising our children to know and appropriately speak the mind of God on a given subject at a given time by the prompting and inspiration of the Holy Spirit.

Goal Exercise

Before you move into the specific training on how prophecy works, please stop and complete this short self-assessment activity:

Give yourself a score between 1 and 10 on how developed you are prophetically, where 1 is not at all, 10 is very regular and effective. By the way, Jesus scores 20 on this scale, so it's okay to give yourself a 9 or a 10 without sounding arrogant!

As you look at your number, what would you like it to be in 3 months time?

What do you want it to be in 1 year?

And how about 3-5 years?

Are you willing to take the training steps necessary to see this come about?

REVELATION: HOW GOD SPEAKS

"This is the greatest grace there is on earth: the possibility of communication between us and God."
Christoph Blumhardt

The mechanics of exactly how God speaks to us is a cause of much fascination, especially when the prophetic gifts are less developed in an individual or a church community.

Let's take a moment to be honest and say that all this has the potential to feel a bit over-mystical and strange! If this is a new area for you, it's okay to acknowledge that fear of man can cause us to hold back from pursuing God and His voice.

In some quarters, for a person to declare that they can hear God speak provokes a response that reflects deep misunderstanding, even mockery. "Okay then Joan of Arc, what's God saying to me now?" Or as Hungarian-American psychiatrist and academic Thomas Szasz wrote in a meme beloved of anti-religion keyboard warriors, "If you talk to God, you are praying; if God talks to you, you have schizophrenia."

To combat these fears and false narratives, we need to ensure that we handle the prophetic gifts in ways that reduce any tendency to unnecessary strangeness. By breaking down the prophetic process into revelation, interpretation and application, we create a pathway to do just that.

- **Revelation:** It is immensely helpful to describe some of the ways God communicates with us, especially when we use language that is as plainly descriptive as possible.

- **Interpretation:** We need to create healthy and robust pathways for evaluation, including being diligent in trying to acknowledge what is probably our own wishful thinking, rather than insisting that everything we say could only be from God.

- **Application:** What to do after receiving a prophecy is all important, and so showing people how to move forward in faith-filled yet common-sense ways is hugely reassuring.

In this chapter, we are going to look at some of the ways that God brings revelation of His love, His thoughts, and His will into our lives.

DON'T FORGET THE WHY

God is speaking all the time, and, because He is God and thus infinitely creative and powerful, He can do so through anything and everything. Clearly we will need a process to distinguish between His thoughts and ours, but before we hit interpretation we must first learn how to 'tune in' to what He is revealing.

When we first step into prophesying, we can become so caught up in the excitement of actually receiving revelation

("I see a rainbow!") that we mislay the purpose of prophecy, and thus short-circuit the process.

Bear in mind that the goal is to gain a sense of what God is saying, so simply sharing "I see a rainbow" isn't particularly helpful (unless the Lord tells you to share only that - which does happen, just don't make that your default). We need to wait in God's presence and ask Him what the rainbow means (e.g. Is that rainbow a sign of God's blessing, or is He about to fulfill a promise, or is Jesus about to show the person where to dig for a pot of gold?!), so that the hearer is not left puzzled as to what on earth is going on.

So as you step further into receiving and sharing revelation, keep in mind that the recipient is most interested in why God is speaking to them (or to use the example above, why He is speaking about rainbows). This will then give them some-thing specific to put through the interpretation and applica-tion stages.

REVELATION

You can divide how God communicates with us into four big pots, which cover most circumstances:

- The Bible
- Seeing stuff
- Hearing stuff
- Knowing stuff

Those may not be very mystical terms, but they do well as a broad foundation!

However, we realize that you'll want more detail than that, so here are 12 of the main ways we have found God releases revelation to people today.

1. BIBLE

Do you ever have that experience when you feel like a phrase, verse, or story from the Bible really stands out to you? You might have read it many times before, but this time it's as if it has just been written for you - right here, right now.

We've both had times too numerous to mention when the text might as well have been printed with Holy Spirit highlighter all around that section! It is as if the words are not to be held captive by print, but somehow they are living and active and speaking personally.

When wanting to encounter God, a classic spiritual discipline is to read the Bible with a heart that is hungry and open to hear from Him. Sometimes it might just be one verse, other times the reading may go on for many chapters. But down the ages Christians have found Scripture to be the most consistent way of hearing from God.

Often we have found that when we are praying for others God will bring to mind a specific verse, character, or story from the Bible that we can share. It becomes a springboard to the other person experiencing encouragement, strengthening, or comfort from God. It is more than simply saying, "Here's a nice verse!", because something more profound occurs - it is as if that verse unlocks something for them.

When we were in our late 20s, Alex was being considered for a position on the staff of a much larger church as a teaching pastor. He was invited to guest preach, and was given free reign to select a passage - which led him into much prayer and concern to find the right text! He ended up feeling strongly led to Isaiah 54, but was never asked about it in advance, so no-one at the interviewing church knew what he'd picked. On the Sunday itself, when he announced and turned to the passage, he was put off his stride because he saw the senior pastor begin talking animatedly to a group of elders near him. Not what you're looking for when you are preaching and a job is on the line! Nevertheless, Alex was too far in by this point, so he boldly challenged the church to respond to specific things in the text, which he felt were God's call over that community. Unbeknown to either of us, one month earlier a famously prophetic guest preacher had spoken from exactly the same passage to the church, and had declared it to be a word over them! Needless to say, Alex was offered the job!

We put the Bible at the number one spot on this list of how God reveals Himself to us because that is the place it holds. The rest of the list is only in a general order, but Scripture is the primary way He speaks.

However, it is not the only way...

2. BRAIN SEEING

One of the most common ways beyond the Bible that people experience God's revelation is through 'seeing' things in their mind's eye.

In the spirit of trying to describe it simply, it is when you 'see' little movies or images on the inside, as Jesus talks to your brain.

Let's try a quick experiment now to illustrate what we mean. Simply close your eyes and picture the front of your home (or a friend's home).

Did something come to mind? The best way to describe the mechanics of what just took place is that you saw your home in your imagination, or your mind's eye. (By the way, when people say 'imagination', it doesn't always mean 'something made up'. Instead, it is a way of describing the internal visually creative aspect of your thinking and feeling.)

Another way of describing it is that this is the part of your brain where you daydream (hopefully not a faculty that you are using right now!)

This is a place where God can give you pictures and visions in your mind. After all, your imagination is no more an aspect of your sinful nature than your thinking is - both are part of God's good creation, and He wants to redeem all aspects of your humanity. So really this is part of the fruit of having an increasingly sanctified imagination.

Jesus seems to model this when He 'sees' Nathaniel sitting under the fig tree before Philip called him (John 1:48-50).

For Alex, this is one of the most common ways he receives revelation. He 'sees' stuff all the time, and finds it so helpful in discerning what God is saying. Sometimes this revelation comes simply as a static image, other times it is like a video clip playing, other times it is specific words (a bit like the news ticker at the bottom of the screen on a news or sports channel!).

3. Brain Hearing

A related way of God revealing Himself is when people 'hear' words on the inside, in their mind.

Focus on the mechanics for a moment: Be quiet for 3 seconds (do that now!), and then see if you can say your name in your head and hear it. In a similar way, that is how people often hear God's voice too. (Obviously, that wasn't being prophetic - we were simply trying to illustrate how this type of internal hearing sounds to you.)

It is probably worth pointing out that this doesn't tend to be a 'volume set to max' kind of experience! A bit like the 'Brain Seeing' section above, there is a choice to be made to pay attention, and then a decision about whether or not these particular words are from God (see two chapters on for more on interpretation).

Nevertheless, it is into our imagination and mind's ear that Jesus will often drop words.

If you are feeling a little anxious at this point - "Gosh, this all sounds a bit flaky" - then let's do a quick theological check.

Do you ever experience tempting thoughts that you know will lead you into sin? And do you ever hear self-condemning words in your mind? Assuming the answer is yes, where do you think those thoughts originate?

We would all agree that those words are not going to be from Jesus. And while some might be self-induced, we all also would likely say that the enemy tempts us to sin, and speaks lies to us.

So here's the theological question: Why do we have more confidence in the enemy's ability to speak to us than we do the Lord Jesus Christ - who is the creator of everything, conqueror of death, defeater of satan, and the greatest lover of your soul?

Jesus loves you so much, and of course he can speak words of life into you directly!

This 'brain hearing' could also be described as a still, small, internal voice. These are sanctified thoughts, which reveal God's heart for a person, community, or situation. This is probably how Ezekiel heard the Lord when the elders sat around him in Ezekiel 14:1-2.

There is also a very common crossover between Brain Seeing and Brain Hearing here. (Don't forget, these are simply our descriptor labels to try to break down something complex and mysterious into everyday language, so the different categories often flow together).

You might well find that God draws your attention to something external, which is physically around you, and speaks to you through that thing. This is especially common when praying for others. For instance, a detail of their clothing or a word on their t-shirt might especially stand out. Alternatively, something that you can see in the room seems to be filled with extra resonance, and you sense on the inside Jesus speaking to you, using that external stimulus as a jumping off point.

As an aside, if this happens to you for someone else, it's not compulsory to explain exactly how you got to the word from Jesus! Sometimes it is helpful, other times you will lose them in the weeds. You are not doing 8th-grade math problems where you need to show all your work!

Recognize that some revelation from Jesus will only makes sense to you.

Think of it like a personal shorthand code between close friends. Jesus will use this private vocabulary (which often conveys emotions as well as facts) to walk you to where He can better release through you what He actually wants to share with that person.

Near the end of this chapter we will give you a prophetic activation exercise that will build upon what we have shared in these early sections on revelation.

4. GUT KNOWING

There is a form of prophetic revelation that can best be described as the experience of simply 'knowing' something about a person or situation, often without any rational evidence.

Generally this 'Gut Knowing' is not related to what you know in the natural about them, so it is not a logical inference. For instance, spotting animal hairs on a woman's coat doesn't mean we start 'prophesying' that she must be a cat-lady!

This is not about a cognitive formulating of pieces of information into a story, but rather the intuition that arises from the Holy Spirit. God can often give us a sense about something - it's difficult to explain exactly how, but you somehow 'know' information that you didn't receive in any way involving your five senses.

A clear Biblical example of this comes in Acts 5:3-4, when Peter prophetically knew about Ananias and Sapphira lying to the church. He didn't know that information other than by a revelation from the Holy Spirit.

One time we were in our small group and talking with people as they arrived, including one lady who was smiling and chatting away. Suddenly I 'knew' that she'd had a huge argument at work that day, and then in my mind's eye I could see her standing there having a big finger-wagging and voice-raising falling out. I also sensed that she was really conflicted about what to do next. So during the evening when the time came for prayer, and giving her lots of opt-outs like, "this might well just be me" / "I wonder if..." (after all, from all externalities this revelation seemed incorrect), I very gently described what I'd felt, and she immediately burst into violent tears. Amidst the sobs she shared that she had indeed had a huge argument with her chairman that day, was really upset about it, realized that she had some repenting to do in order to move forward, but was (understandably) annoyed with him as well.

As the group ministered to her, it was a powerful example of Jesus bringing revelation in order to bring comfort and wisdom to someone. Don't forget, in spite of the positive tone of the prophetic gifts, they can indeed bring tears and strong emotions, as Jesus wants to minister to those deep places in us.

We have both had numerous times when we've just known something that seems almost counter-intuitive. Sometimes this can be to do with a person's motives, or perhaps a direction that the Lord wants us to take, or the spiritual realities of a situation (we will cover lots on this in our book on deliverance and spiritual warfare), or even a sin that is being hidden.

Of course, WHAT you do with that revelation and interpretation is another thing altogether! That is what we will cover in the chapter on application.

5. FEELINGS

God created us to benefit from emotions, and at times we can 'catch' what God is saying through them. In other words, if we learn to pay attention to subtle changes, Jesus can speak to us through our emotions.

For instance, have you ever met someone who seems to carry a deep sadness (in spite of how their face looks)? Or walked into a home that almost enfolds you with a divine peace? Or perhaps made a decision and felt a reality-defying confidence that this is the correct pathway for you to take? Those might well be indicators from God about something He wants you to know.

As we go through life, we naturally have emotional responses to people and places. Jesus can elevate those feelings to a higher level, whereby the Spirit of God is actively communicating to us. We can learn to recognize that not all emotions come from within us, but can also be externally driven by God (or the enemy). This then becomes a clue about something to which our attention should be drawn, and we then discern what sort of response is needed.

Speaking personally, for us a good example of this comes as we make decisions. Often we will ask God for direction, and the way He chooses to steer us will on occasion be through our feelings, rather than simply speaking to our logic. For instance, when Hannah was pregnant with our sons, we sought the Lord for what their names should be (believing that naming is a prophetic act). With each child God highlighted a particular name (and its meaning) to Hannah, and did so by giving her a strong feeling about, and resonance with, that name.

It is interesting that many evangelicals seem fearful of relying on emotions in any significant way, as if somehow feelings are inherently less redeemable than our minds. Not only is this dualistic worldview unbiblical, it will also result in us missing out on some of God's revelation coming to or through us.

Paul tells us in Colossians 3:15 to *"let the peace of Christ rule in your hearts."* The word for 'rule' could be translated as referee or direct. In other words, as we lean into a decision, we are to look for the presence - or absence - of the peace of Jesus as an indicator that we are headed in the right direction. That is not a mind-assessed thing, but rather a situation where we are to pay attention to redeemed emotions.

6. OUR BODIES

God seems to enjoy reminding us that He made our bodies, and that He can speak through them to us as well.

2 Chronicles 5 records the consecration of the temple built by Solomon, and at the climax of the ceremony and worship we read:

> "The trumpeters and singers joined together to praise and thank the Lord with one voice. They raised their voices, accompanied by trumpets, cymbals, and musical instruments, in praise to the Lord: 'For He is good; His loving devotion endures forever.' Then the temple, the house of the Lord, was filled with a cloud so that the priests could not stand there to minister because of the cloud; for the glory of the Lord filled the house of God." (v.13-14)

What an incredible experience! We have seen and experienced milder versions of this, when the presence of God is so heavy on an individual that they can not stand in the presence of God. He is revealing His weighty glory and goodness, and inviting them into a special time of closeness and encounter with Him.

Another way God can reveal His will through our bodies comes when we have sudden unexpected aches and pains that reveal what's going on in someone else's body. This tends to be a revelation that is given to people to share publicly, so that those who have that condition can grow in faith for healing. We explore this topic in far more detail in our book, *Operating in Words of Knowledge and Wisdom*.

• • •

7. Dreams

Have you ever had a dream that you believe was from God?

Your dream life can a significant area of spiritual action and growth. For some this is a common thing to experience - we even have friends who ended up married (happily!) after one of them had a dream where Jesus revealed that He wanted them to marry!

It is important to notice from Scripture that God loves to speak through dreams. The Bible records around 320 dreams from God, so that definitely counts as a pattern of which we are to be aware!

In the Muslim majority nations, especially those that are most hostile to Christians, one of the main ways people are currently coming to faith is through dreams where Jesus appears and speaks directly to that person. We have heard countless stories of this taking place, and each one is both beautiful and awe-inspiring.

As Westerners we tend to look down on dreams as something a bit weak or second rate, but actually they are a significant way for God to minister, speak, and impact us.

As we've noted earlier on similar themes, if we recognize nightmares can come from enemy, why not be happy asserting that some dreams come from the Lord?

Job 33:14-18 speaks clearly to this matter.

> *"For God does speak - now one way, now another - though no one perceives it. In a dream, in a vision of the night, when deep sleep falls on people as they slumber in their beds, he may speak in their ears and terrify them with warnings, to turn them from wrongdoing and keep them from pride, to preserve them from the pit, their lives from perishing by the sword."*

It seems to be that sometimes God has to wait until we are asleep before He can get a word in edgewise! For others, it is during sleep that there is enough quiet and openness to allow Him to work on hearts and attitudes.

While our bodies may be resting, our spirits are very much awake and engaged with the spiritual realm.

Of course, not all dreams come from God - as we noted, some are from evil spirits, and many are simply our internal systems processing an excess of late night cheese, wine and movies! When we do recognize a dream is from God, the key remains the interpretation (the Bible shows wicked people receiving dreams from God — so simply receiving one doesn't make you prophetic!). We'll talk about this more in the chapter on interpretation, where you'll find a special section to give you some guidelines on the interpretation of dreams.

8. Creation

The Creator can be found in His creation! Romans 1 reminds us that His creation is designed to inspire and stir us to encounter Him. In fact, according to Paul, God's invisible qualities are so clearly displayed in creation that we are without excuse for at least making some sort of reverent response to His revelation.

Probably you'll have heard lost friends say things like, "Being outdoors hiking/ gardening/ surfing/ running is my church." To them it sounds all spiritual and meaningful, even if we know it is more akin to worshipping the creation rather than the Creator.

Nevertheless, it is a jumping off place. All of us have had those moments where we stand breath-taken by a sunset in a beautiful spot. That can be a place that not only stirs us to worship, but also an environment that is more conducive to hearing God's voice.

Creation is a place where we can experience God speaking to us, often through some of the pathways mentioned earlier.

9. Physical Seeing and Hearing

As you grow in the prophetic, one of the ways that God might bring revelation to you is externally through your eyeballs and ears.

An external vision is where you can see superimposed words or images put over what you are seeing in the natural. The best way we can describe this is that it is kind of like the augmented reality you might find on a phone app! For instance, we have often 'seen' words externally projected over a person, which might describe something going on in their life or which reveals something about them.

In the Bible, Ezekiel's vision of the valley of dry bones (Ezekiel 37:1-14) is an example of an external vision, while Acts 16:9 records when Paul had a similar experience: *"During the night Paul had a vision of a man of Macedonia standing and begging him, 'Come over to Macedonia and help us.'"*

Similarly, God can reveal Himself through external sounds. One of our craziest experiences of this came when Alex was preaching on revival, and specifically was comparing it to the Holy Spirit coming as a heavy rain that brings refreshing. As he said those words, suddenly the sound of heavy rain hammering down on the church roof filled the building. It was so unexpected that someone put their head outside... and it was a cloudless night! What was even more strange was that not everyone heard the sound - to some it was deafening, while others had no idea what the rest of us were talking about!

This sort of external hearing of sounds appears in the Bible, such as when Elijah hears the sound of heavy rain (1 Kings 18:41), or David's army is commanded to attack only once they hear the sound of marching in the tops of the poplar trees (2 Samuel 5:24).

Other times people might hear the voice of God audibly and externally. Generally this seems to come to people when the revelation is something significant and weighty (think more of a calling scenario), but of course we don't want to restrict Him to that. Biblical examples include the Ten Commandments being given, the baptism of Jesus, and the call of Samuel (in that latter case, the voice seems only to have been audible to him).

Finally, sometimes people see Jesus come to them in physical form. Hannah had that experience as a child aged 5 (when, early one morning, Jesus calmly appeared to her in her bedroom), and it was a profound influence on her throughout her childhood. While it is not an everyday sort of thing, it does happen, and of course is a humbling and richly signifi-cant encounter.

10. Angels

Their very name means 'messenger', and thus there are stories throughout the Bible and Christian history of angels bringing messages from God. We need to make room in our understanding for holy, intelligent, (generally) invisible, spiri-tual beings other than God.

For instance, just look at the instances of angelic action throughout the book of Acts. There we see angels orches-trating multiple jail breaks (5:18-20, and then 12:6-10), giving travel instructions that lead to a salvation conversation (8:26), appearing to a spiritually hungry yet lost centurion (10:3-6), executing Herod for taking praise that is due only to God (and in a fabulously gory twist, arranging for a bunch of body-eating worms to complete the job!) (12:23), and standing alongside Paul to assure protection to 276 people on an otherwise doomed ship (27:23-24).

Angels have not disappeared since the Bible. We know a number of people who have personally experienced angelic intervention to rescue them from dangerous situations. They also continue their role as messengers, bringing revelation to individuals and offering guidance. For obvious reasons these stories don't tend to be shared much, but that doesn't mean angels are now all retired!

11. CIRCUMSTANCES

God can speak to us, and direct us, through the circumstances of our lives. From our perspective this generally feels like God is opening and closing the doors of opportunity, and certainly that is something all of us will have prayed at some point when faced with decisions. However, just because something doesn't work out for you, that doesn't mean God has closed the door - it could be the enemy at work, or our own lack of maturity or patience!

Other times God's hand on our lives appears as a supernatural incident that correlates with natural events. These appear to us like patterns, which eventually we spot and realize that God could be speaking through them.

For instance, our whole process of moving to the US from England was surrounded by rain and floods (including our possessions almost being flooded out of the storage facility before being shipped, record snowfall on our interview week, huge rain as we arrived at our new home) - and that tied in with multiple prophetic words about God bringing rains of blessing upon our lives in that major transition.

12. ANYTHING!

We have given you a list that we have tried to reverse engineer from what we have seen, but of course God is endlessly creative. He loves to speak and communicate, and you might know of testimonies that are unbelievable aside from your trust of that person.

Some other ways that we could talk about include:

- Movies and TV shows — Lots of people have seen parables and deeper meanings in these visual stories that they know are the Holy Spirit talking to them.

- Music — Perhaps related to God speaking to our emotions as well as our minds, God indeed speaks through music and song (for instance, we have heard testimony of Foreigner's classic love song "I Want to Know What Love Is" being the pivotal moment in someone coming to faith in Christ!)

- Smell — We have smelt the fragrance of Jesus on a number of occasions (which speaks to us of God's reassuring presence and hand upon a particular direction), while there is also a distinctive demonic smell (which, by the way, is often like sulphur/ rotten eggs, as you might expect!)

- Actions — Sometimes God leads us to do certain actions that carry prophetic weight (e.g. symbolically 'cutting' a person free from masonic insignia), perhaps revealing something that God is doing in the spiritual. For a biblical example, check out Agabus binding Paul's hands with his belt to signify his upcoming imprisonment (Acts 21:10-14)

In summary, there are LOTS of ways to sense what God is communicating to us. Some are more common, and the earlier bullet points above pick up on this. Nevertheless, invite and be open to God speaking to you in a variety of creative ways — He loves that sort of challenge!

We have friends who, while pastoring a church, found that the big highway billboard near their church building continually spoke to their church's situation over a several year period. Sometimes the advertisements simply encouraged, other times they provoked or even warned, but they were able to list an incredible range of correlations between the two. Strange, but fun, and how very like Jesus to do something so ingenious and personal!

Activation Exercise

This would be a good time to try out the 'Tray Exercise' in the *Activation Exercises* chapter of this book. It is a fun thing to do, and a good way to see some of the ways in which God speaks to you.

The heart of
a prophetic person
should be
humble and
teachable.

HOW TO SHARE REVELATION

Before we dive into interpreting what has been shared, we want to give you some guidance on how to actually share a prophecy.

Most of us will fall into one of two pitfalls: being incredibly nervous and hesitant ("This sounds so arrogant to say God might have spoken to me about you"), or being brash and insensitive ("Thus saith the Lord: this is a life-changing revelation!") Our hope is to position you in the middle ground!

HOW CAN I BE SURE IT'S GOD?

The question of certainty is front and center for all of us as we try to hear from God. In the next chapter we'll focus on how you weigh and interpret a prophetic word, but here are a few quick pointers for self-assessment, as you filter what you are sensing. Think of these as internal markers of what a prophetic word might 'feel' like on the inside:

- Revelation from God carries greater love than your own thoughts. It is also characterized by a deeper wisdom, insight, and kindness. There will be times where you'll think to yourself, "Wow! That is good stuff!" - and you'll know there is no way you could possibly have dreamed that up yourself.

- Something that is from God will often cause a resonating response within you. That might be a sense of holy reverence, or great excitement and expectation, or conviction of sin (which comes with hope and not condemnation), or a deep peace that might well be in contrast to the circumstances.

- A prophetic word also carries within it the seed of faith to see it through to fulfillment. What we mean is that when someone embraces a word, there is a release of strength, perseverance, and desire to follow the Lord on the pathway that He is highlighting, in spite of any obstacles.

- While we might need to wait in God's presence for a little while to hear from Him, don't forget that a prophetic word will usually come simply and easily. The actual revelation tends to gently float down upon us like a landing butterfly, rather than coming as an overwhelming flood of raw power that knocks us off our feet. Of course, while that is not a universal law, it is a good rule of thumb. For many starting out in the prophetic, the challenge is to recognize that revelation is more intuitive than cognitive in nature - it is art more than science. It is not our frenzied self-effort that brings the word from God. Rather, as we simply learn to wait upon Him, we are attentive to the different ways in which He might communicate. And if nothing comes, that is not on us to resolve.

- The voice of Jesus will have a net-positive impact -

strengthening, comforting, and encouraging, even when bringing challenge or change. The devil's voice will be net negative - once you are past the initial 'high' of embracing a temptation, then the enemy's true hand is shown: it is confusing, discouraging, entrapping, and can leave you worried or obsessed. Jesus summarized the contrast this way: *"The thief comes only to steal and kill and destroy; I have come that they may have life, and have it to the full."* (John 10:10)

- Bear in mind that the enemy will be trying to sow lies and confusion. Immediately after you get some revelation that you think might be from the Lord, if you suddenly doubt that it is genuinely God speaking, remember that this self-questioning could be from the devil. In Mark 4:14-15 we read that after God sows the seed, the enemy tries to snatch it away. Don't let the thief disillusion you or tempt you to give up. If you keep pressing in and asking Jesus to reveal more of Himself to you, He surely will!

SOME BASIC RULES FOR SHARING PROPHECY

As you start out in sharing revelation, we have a couple of basic rules that we strongly enforce - and would encourage you to operate by them as well.

These are not to quench the Spirit, but rather to create a safe space for people to grow in their gifts in ways that are not pastorally destructive.

There might come a time when some of these restrictions (#1 and #4) can be loosened, but that will only be in the context of a proven prophetic ministry that is thoroughly accountable. We will talk about this in our book, *Building a Prophetic Culture.*

So here are some of our core rules:

1. "No Dates, No Mates, No Direction, No Correction!"

A. Do NOT prophesy dates for when longed for things will occur (such as babies, a marriage, the end of financial troubles, etc). People are far too vulnerable in such circumstances, and immense harm can occur to a hearer who is not mature in Christ.

We have close friends who were trying to conceive a child for a number of years, and they shared with us how someone (who was seasoned prophetically and should have known better) prayed over them and declared, 'Mark your calendar for 9 months from now, you will be holding your baby.' Over a year later, that had not happened. Another time the wife was told, 'The Lord says, "If you'd just change your attitude then you would get your baby".' Such stories should shock us - and make us determined not to see the prophetic gifts abused in such heartbreaking ways.

So when someone with an emotionally charged need seeks you out for prayer, be aware that, unless you are a Vulcan or a robot, your own emotions will pick up on that deep longing in front of you. You will long to provide tangible hope, possibly including a date, in order to help and love them. But understand this: even though you'll claim your motives are pure, what you are sensing is not the Lord but rather your own heart-angst.

Instead, grow up, get some self-control, and don't you dare start issuing dates or similar false reassurances! Prayer ministry and prophesying over others is a privilege, and it is not about you. Remember that the #1 need for these dear emotionally wrung out people in front of you is to experience the Father's love - which will not be the case if you simply speak out of your own emotional immaturity.

If you do sense something specific about a date or similar, do not even hint at this to them. Simply record it later in your journal - if it proves to be true, you can always show the person you prayed for at a later date, and if you were wrong, you can learn from the experience without inflicting pastoral harm.

B. Do NOT give out names of future marriage partners. ("I really think that God is showing me that you and N are going to end up together.) Just don't do this. Ever.

C. Do NOT tell someone what their major life decisions need to be. "I see you running your own business in France, and the Lord says, 'Sell everything and go all in'!" Even if you are right (unlikely unless you are incredibly gifted), heavy-handed directiveness takes away from that person the vital need to hear God for themselves on such a decision. The prophetic gifts are to help, not hinder, disciple-making, and people must learn to draw closer to God themselves, not be spoon fed by others.

In this specific example, you could instead say, "This could just be me, but I keep feeling that there is something significant about France and your career. Does that make any sense to you?" This is not directive in any way, but might be a helpful confirmatory word if God is indeed giving them a calling to move there.

D. Do NOT correct their behavior via a 'prophecy.' If someone has a really annoying habit and you then have the opportunity to pray over them, guess what you are tempted to prophesy??! "I feel like God would have you stop complaining all the time/ picking on that particular person/ doing that weird tutting noise when you start speaking."

Prophecy is not the place to raise those issues. Instead, if it is something that you need to address, talk to them in a regular conversation, and don't manipulate them with Jesus language.

2. NEVER SAY, "THUS SAITH THE LORD!"

Firstly, don't use old fashioned language when prophesying. It makes you sound more strange, not more spiritual!

Secondly, when you share a word with someone, always give them permission to weigh and reject it. For us this means that we will ALWAYS add caveats before and during sharing - *"I would encourage you to weigh this/ this might well be the cheese I ate last night, but I wonder if... / I wonder if Jesus might be saying to you.../ I sense God could be showing me that.../"* and so on.

If it has been an especially strong prophecy, at the end we might reinforce this sentiment, by saying, *"Please weigh this, and chat about it with someone with whom you are accountable, because this might well be me."* We do this even when we are internally highly certain what we are sharing is from the Lord, because it is part of honoring the individual as having intrinsic value, as well as not forming co-dependent relationships that hinder their discipleship.

3. DON'T BE THE PROPHECY ENFORCER

There are some people who prophesy and then want lots of updates over the subsequent weeks as to how that receiver is enacting what was shared. Unless you are in an existing accountable relationship with them, this is really unhelpful, because you are using a gift of the Spirit to promote your own human authority. Plus you will quickly become really irritating to them! We've had this happen to us and, honestly, it is SO annoying - we've ended up avoiding people as a result!

Again, leave them to weigh the word and to decide what to do next, if anything. Your role is not to be Jesus' enforcer!

Early on in our marriage Alex prayed that the Lord would help him forget the prophetic words he shared, unless the Lord specifically wanted him to remember something. Even to this day he will recall very few words - which actually has enabled him to minister to many and subsequently be unaffected by what the Lord has revealed.

4. Do Stick To 1 Corinthians 14:3

Memorize this key verse: *"The one who prophesies speaks to people for their strengthening, encouraging and comfort"* (1 Corinthians 14:3).

If you stick to those three outcomes when you prophecy - that the other person is strengthened, encouraged and comforted - then you won't go far wrong.

This will then create a safe environment for you to practice the prophetic gifts, since that is what you need to do. These wonderful gifts don't fall into our laps fully formed, and so by obeying this Scripture then you can have room to make mistakes, learn and grow.

TIMING

As you begin to hear God's revelation more clearly, one of the barriers to effective prophetic ministry will be timing. Put simply, just because God shows you something, that doesn't mean He wants you to share it!

The question of timing is not one that can be set by universally applicable rules, since every situation is unique. But please do not assume that there should be as short a gap as possible between you receiving revelation and you sharing it.

So why would Jesus show you something about a person or situation, yet want you to remain quiet?

Consider this: perhaps He is showing you something not to share with others, and not for your ego to feel on the inside track, but rather to ask you to pray.

The Lord is looking for faithful women and men with whom He can share, inviting you into an intercessory partnership.

It could be that this is a one-off prayer, or maybe God wants you to intercede for them over a longer period of time. Just know that sometimes you will be given a word for someone or a situation but will never be released to share it. However, if you are faithful in prayer, tremendous Kingdom advancing things can happen out of that revelation! Our job is to be obedient with what we have been given.

ACCOUNTABILITY

The heart of a prophetic person should be humble and teachable, with a genuine desire to be accountable. This requires us laying down the unrealistic expectation that everything we hear and share will be 100% from God - that simply won't be the case.

Never confuse anointing with maturity. God may speak to you with tremendous clarity, but that doesn't automatically make you mature in Christ or no longer subject to your leaders. Like any gift, there is an aspect of prophecy that is a skill in which you can develop and grow - but it takes time, effort, practice, and outside coaching.

Due to its ability to cut through to someone's core sense of identity, prophecy is a gift that requires pastoring. This means that we should invite input, and ensure that we ourselves are always under godly leadership. This is important for our own growth, for the health of the church family, and for the protection of God's reputation.

Kris Vallotton writes, "When poor or bad supernatural ministry goes unchecked or unchallenged by other mature believers, it creates a culture where people lose faith in the miraculous."

Some of our rules listed above are designed to create guard rails to guide prophetic people further into maturity, and to minimize the damage that a runaway prophetic voice can inflict. Remember that Paul says in 1 Corinthians 14:32, *"The spirits of prophets are subject to the control of prophets."* This means that we should be exercising self-control - which is one of the fruits of the same Spirit who releases the prophetic revelation.

In our book *Building a Prophetic Culture* we share a lot more detail on how to do this in practice. But for now, remember that just because we sense something is from God that doesn't mean we are released simply to blurt it out regardless of impact.

IT'S ALL ABOUT LOVE

"If I have the gift of prophecy and can fathom all mysteries and all knowledge, and if I have a faith that can move mountains, but do not have love, I am nothing."
I Corinthians 13:2

The key to effective prophetic ministry will always be to operate out of love — for God, and for the recipient. You will face all sorts of situations and contexts as you grow in the prophetic, and at times you won't be clear how to respond. Yet if you seek to do everything out of a heart of love, you will be in a great place to minister fruitfully.

INTERPRETATION: HOW TO TEST A PROPHECY

When I (Alex) was at seminary, and before Hannah and I had met, my substantial vacations were spent working for a Christian travel company. Whether it was skiing in the Alps, or summers on Europe's beaches and tourist hotspots, the company was a magnet for young adults - helped by its renown for birthing romance and marriage!

At breakfast on day two of a 14-day trip I was leading to Italy, one young woman asked if she could have a chat with me that morning. Later, as she and I sat down outside a cafe on the Tuscany coast, while much of the group enjoyed a beach day around us, I was completely unprepared for what would come next.

> "Alex, I wanted to meet with you because I feel that Jesus has said that you and I are going to get married," she declared.

> "ARRRRRRRRGGGGGGGGGGGGGGHHHHHHHHHHH-HHHHHHH" I screamed (on the inside).

> "Well," I stuttered, after picking up my jaw from the

sidewalk, "that's ever so sweet of you, but, erm, Jesus hasn't said anything to me about that!"

After promising her that I'd pray about it, I immediately told the other two members of my team. Once they'd stopped laughing, the rest of the two weeks was spent with them watching my back and 'stepping in' whenever I looked in danger of being cornered by my admirer!

THE DILEMMA OF INTERPRETATION

That story wonderfully illustrates the dilemma of interpretation.

Just what do you say when someone announces, 'Jesus says we're going to marry each other'? After all, if we believe that God speaks, isn't the choice of a marriage partner one of those things that we might well expect Him to have some helpful views on?

As an aside, sometimes God will reveal that you're going to marry a particular person! If that does happen, the mature response is not to share it, but rather to privately file away the thought, pray about it, and if the marriage does happen you can share the prophetic word afterwards (or at least after the engagement) as wonderful confirmation!

At a more mundane level, we face the same questions in the smaller moments of life. As we taught our sons how to hear God's voice, there were times when they would try it on to see if they could benefit from this new vocabulary. "I was praying and I felt like it's okay for me to stay up late and watch this movie", came the 10-year-old plea for access to the promised land of PG-13 action adventures!

Not everything that pops into your head is from God, even when you pray and are being sincere.

There are times when you will simply have been incorrect in your assessment that an idea was divine revelation.

But don't worry — that is okay!

In order to grow in the prophetic gifts you will need to stretch yourself and test the boundaries. Sometimes you will be completely wrong, more often it might be that you heard something from God but then added your own spin or bias, or perhaps you didn't have the courage to truly speak out what you sensed, for fear of the response.

Of course, we don't want to be loose cannons going around firing off pseudo-spiritual broadsides, so it is important to have some objective, shared ways to weigh and assess a prophetic revelation.

HOW DO WE WEIGH WHAT WE HEAR?

In a punchy few verses in 1 Thessalonians 5:19-22, we read:

> *"Do not quench the Spirit. Do not treat prophecies with contempt but test them all; hold on to what is good, reject every kind of evil."*

Paul is giving us a bold and clear call to be open to prophetic gifts, and to be wise in weighing what is shared (which implies that prophetic revelation in the church will rarely be 100% correct, and will always require testing.)

Here are six yardsticks that you can use to help you weigh a prophecy: Scripture, Love, Speaker, Wisdom, Resonance, and Fulfillment.

1. SCRIPTURE: *Does it Line Up with the Bible?*

Egyptian hieroglyphics are an ancient and mysterious language, the meaning of which became lost to humanity from about 400AD onwards. Down the centuries many valiant attempts had been made to translate them, but none bore any success... until July 15, 1799.

By then Egypt was a conquest ground for the armies of France's fast rising General Napoleon. On that particular day, a group of his troops were building foundations for a fort near the town of Rosetta. As they dug they unearthed a stone covered in inscriptions, which were later dated to 196BC. The text was written in three distinct languages - Hieroglyphs (the language of the Egyptian priests), Demotic (the old language of the people), and Ancient Greek (the language of Egypt's rulers at that time.)

Scholars were quickly able to hypothesize that this stone was created to communicate the same decree in the three languages of the day - and thus the Rosetta Stone was the translation key to unlocking the mysteries of hieroglyphics. And so that proved to be.

As followers of Jesus, the Bible is the Rosetta Stone for translating every other way in which we claim God might speak. It is the objective yardstick to which we turn to measure and assess all other words. If someone claims to have a word from God, it must always line up with both the teaching and the tone of the Bible.

While all this might sound fairly obvious, it is amazing how many struggle with this principle.

When Alex was a young pastor in his 20s, he had to confront a much older man who was having a full blown affair. Looking Alex in the eye, the man said, "I know it's not the usual thing, but God has clearly said that it's okay for me to be having this relationship, because of my wife being so diffi-cult and not understanding me and my needs." To which back came the response, "Well, let's go look in the Bible shall we? Because last time I checked, not committing adultery was still in God's Top 10!"

Of course, not every situation will be as black and white as that. Sometimes you will listen to a possible prophecy and it will feel out of sync with the Bible less on specific theology and more on its tone or texture. Put another way, it just won't sound like the sort of thing that Jesus would say. It is important in those moments to do the discipline of putting words to that unease (if for no other reason than to help the person sharing the word to grow).

Scripture is the Rosetta Stone through which everything else is translated. It is God-breathed and is the primary way God reveals Himself to us. Therefore, if someone shares what they think is a revelation from God that is in conflict with the Bible, their word is judged not to be from God. The Bible always wins!

Ask yourself: Does this revelation line up with what the Bible teaches and reveals about God?

2. LOVE: Does it Reflect the Heart of God?

"Follow the way of love and eagerly desire gifts of the Spirit, especially prophecy." (1 Corinthians 14:1)

The essence of prophecy is love. It is a revelation of the heart of the Father for a person, community or situation - and God is a loving Dad!

A prophetic word should be good news to the hearer. This doesn't mean it must all be rainbows topped with deliriously happy unicorns - there are times when a prophecy can bring high challenge and a weighty sense of seriousness. Yet any word from God will flow with an undercurrent of His great love for the recipient. **The fruit will be that the recipient is**

brought closer to God's Father heart, and very often to the rest of God's family, the church.

Even when a word is bringing challenge about an area that requires repentance and change, the message should stir conviction rather than condemnation. Christ sets us free from the law of sin and death, and so we receive grace in the midst of the challenge, because it is through the Spirit's empowering that we can step into a new and better way of living.

Ask yourself: Does this revelation feel like it carries the love of the Father?

3. SPEAKER: Do They Have an Agenda?

One of the ways we weigh a word is to look at who is sharing it. What fruit is being borne in the speaker's life? Are they the sort of person through whom Jesus might choose to share this revelation?

Generally this is not going to be an issue, since in our experience most people are not trying to do anything other than hesitantly share what they sense might be from God. However, there are moments where something feels off about the person sharing.

Perhaps you know enough about their character or lifestyle to wonder if they really can hear clearly from Jesus (although we must be careful not to fall into the trap of the Pharisees, who believed that anyone less holy than them could not possibly be used by God.) This is not about being qualified to prophesy by human standards, but by God's. We have watched 7 and 8 year olds speak meaningful prophetic words over adults (so it's not about age or life maturity), and heard church elders claim to be speaking for God in ways that have set off all sorts of warning signals.

There have been a few occasions when we've listened to someone speaking, and on the inside our spirits are saying, "I really don't trust you and your agenda." It is as if someone has been 'prophesying' their own agenda over us or a situation, taking their desires and wrapping them in Jesus-ey language.

A more common version of this occurs when someone knows the details of a situation, wants to speak prophetically over those involved, and doesn't have the self-awareness to heavily filter what they hear, or at the very least openly acknowledge their own biases or preferences. When we have found ourselves in that place of praying over a good friend who has already shared a lot of information, we work hard to be open about our flesh desires, and add lots of qualifying clauses to whatever revelation we share. **If we know we are going to be praying and prophesying over someone, often times we will stop them sharing much information with us in advance, which helps keep things far cleaner.**

Again, having to question the speaker's heart is not the norm — most mistakes come out of a genuine and good desire to bless others, without any other agenda at work. However, it would be naive not to pay attention if we sense some other motives at work in the person who is bringing a prophecy.

Ask yourself: Does the one sharing come with an agenda?

4. WISDOM: Do OTHER WISE PEOPLE THINK IT'S FROM GOD?

The New Testament picture of prophecy shifts the responsibility onto the community to weigh what is being shared. In 1 Corinthians 14:29 we read,*"Two or three prophets should speak, and the others should weigh carefully what is said."*

There is something about doing prophecy in community that helps mitigate against disorder, immaturity or heresy.

In practice, this doesn't mean that every time someone shares with you a simple word of encouragement that you must rush off to arrange a two hour meeting with an elder or a pastor! Part of maturity is learning how to weigh a lot of the more everyday personal stuff for ourselves, and simply allowing it to encourage and feed us.

However, there will be weightier words that are shared with you — perhaps in a church gathering, whether that's public worship on Sunday or, as Paul is thinking of in Corinth, in homes - which you'll want to seek counsel on. The main place for this processing will probably be with your spouse and/or your accountability partner, as they know you best and can operate as a sounding board for what emerges. It can be helpful sometimes to draw in a few others, depending on relationships and your state of mind. Clearly one of the options will be your spiritual leaders, since those who have oversight over us from God are often given insight into us from God.

As you share, allow them to ask questions about the process, what was shared, how you are understanding it, and what your response is (more on application in the next chapter). How much do they feel this word is from God? How do they see it lining up with other parts of your story, calling and gifts? What do they recommend doing about it? What is their wisdom for you on timing, application, etc?

Ask yourself: Do those in your place of spiritual account-ability agree this word is from God?

5. RESONANCE: *Does it 'Feel' Right?*

If our only test for a prophetic word was 'does it feel right?', we would quite rightly have some concern at the potential for abuse. However, as part of a more robust list that begins with Scripture, that intuitive gut check is actually a very helpful tool as we seek to interpret a revelation.

A prophetic word should stir a 'Yes and Amen!' in the spirit of the recipient — even if they don't fully understand it yet, or they know it is challenging. A prophecy should bear witness in the spirit of the recipient. **This means that the Holy Spirit inside you is resonating with what is shared, giving you an internal peace that what is being shared is from God.**

When something is shared that people are processing, a ques-tion we find helpful to ask is whether what has been shared sounds like the sort of thing that Jesus would say.

We have been in rooms where someone has shared something that simply felt funky — and very interestingly, almost everyone had the same sense, even if they weren't sure if/how to share that. In fact, we've even had non-Christian friends with us in such scenarios, and they are surprisingly receptive to the 'does that sound like something Jesus would say' framework.

In Philippians 4:7 we are promised that *"the peace of God, which transcends all understanding, will guard your hearts and your minds in Christ Jesus."* One of the tests we look for is how the peace of God is steering us in response to a prophecy. It might be a challenging word, but underneath there should be a sense of the Holy Spirit bringing us peace, reminding us that He is with us and will lead us forward.

When the two disciples on the road to Emmaus (Cleopas and probably Mary, his wife) process their experience of hearing the resurrected Jesus explain the Scriptures, they comment, *"Were not our hearts burning within us while he talked with us on the road and opened the Scriptures to us?"* (Luke 24:32) Our experience is that on many occasions the heart does indeed burn when we hear a word from the Lord.

Ask yourself: Does this word feel like the sort of thing Jesus would say?

6. FULFILLMENT: Does it Prove True?

One of the things that prophecy does is to release revelation about things from the past that are hidden, or things for today and the future that will come to pass. So one of the tests of that aspect of prophecy is to ask whether or not it proves true.

A simple way of doing that assessment is to ask:

1. Is it correct (if the word is hindsight focused)?
2. Is it an accurate analysis (if the word is insight focused)?
3. Does it come true (if the word is foresight focused)?

Sometimes it is a simple matter to test whether or not the speaker shared something true. If it is, that is a cause of thanksgiving and faith building!

On those times when what is shared is not true, a couple of responses might be helpful.

- If you are the recipient of the word, is it totally incorrect or just partially so? For instance, someone speaks about your childhood car, and they name the right model, but have the wrong color. In that case, stay with the bigger word and see if that minor incorrect detail is overshadowed by the greater weight of far more other parts of the word being accurate and faith building. What often happens as we share prophetic insight is that in our enthusiasm we share a little bit more than we were meant to (in this case, the car color). We would not regard that as anything very worrying, and more an opportunity for the person sharing to receive a little feedback that helps them sharpen their revelation focus.

- If what is shared is clearly wrong, then we would choose to bless the person for their desire to hear from God, and ask the Lord to remove its impact from us, so that it doesn't shape our thinking or expectations. If you are in relationship with the one who shared, pray about whether, and how, to feed back to them. It could be they prophesied over you as part of an official church ministry team, in which case the team leader might be a good person to speak with as well.

- If you find someone regularly sharing spiritual junk, then that is more serious, and you should definitely feed that back to their team or church leaders. They will need to undergo more training and closer supervision. We will cover a lot more on these matters in our book, *Building a Prophetic Culture*.

Ask yourself: Is this revelation true?

A WORD ON INTERPRETING DREAMS

Simply having meaningful dreams does not make us prophetic or even worth listening to. The Bible shows some very ungodly people having dreams! The prophetic task is actually in the interpretation.

Our contemporary culture is packed with all sorts of schools of thought on dream interpretation — just a quick browse in a bookstore will reveal the interest in this topic, many of which claim a spiritual foundation. In response, some Christians run away from any attempt to interpret dreams that feel like they carry spiritual depth, which is just as mistaken as turning to false religion to understand a dream's meaning.

To help you discern more clearly, here are a few specific suggestions in addition to the broader interpretation list above.

- As you look back at a dream, pay attention not simply to what you saw but also how you felt, since Jesus might well be revealing something important through your emotions.

- Don't over-interpret! Dreams are pretty crazy places, and it is extremely unlikely that you are meant to be dissecting every single image or moment. Generally there is a big idea, or destination, through which God reveals something to you.

- Dreams in particular are an area where we need to *"test the spirits."* 1 John 4:1-6 speaks clearly to this principle. As you look back on a dream, did it draw you closer to God? Did it inspire you to honor and worship Him? Or, by contrast, was it something that had little that was edifying about it, and instead seemed to tempt you away from pursuing the path of following Jesus?

- If God begins to speak to you regularly through dreams, you might be like some people we know who have ended up with a kind of dream language that God uses to communicate with them. If they see a certain thing in the dream, that is an interpretative key later on (for example - and please note that this might NOT be the same code for you - we have friends who when they dream about vehicles or transportation know that probably represents ministry). Others know that God speaks to them through particular numbers, colors (e.g. white represents purity), or places. Some of those shorthands make sense when explained to other people, while others are unique and highly particular to that person. So watch out for patterns and things that God seems to show to you in dreams, and over time you might begin to develop a bit of shorthand like this.

- It is important not to rest upon a formula, but rather the present voice of God. As Joseph notes before Pharaoh, God is the one who reveals the answers we seek. Patterns and a shorthand dream language are useful, but don't allow them to take the place of pursuing God personally each time. Never substitute the rule of thumb for actually seeking the Lord!

- At a practical level, we both keep pen and paper beside our beds, so that if the Lord either awakens us in the night with a word, or we recognize that we have had a meaningful dream, we can then record it immediately. **To be honest, simply thinking, "I'll** remember that one in the morning" and then rolling over and going back to sleep almost always results in a forgotten dream or revelation!

GROW IN WEIGHING PROPHECY

When you are starting out in the prophetic, your focus will tend to be drawn to the methodology of receiving revelation. As you become more mature, though, it will be important to put more attention onto the interpretation.

In the situation where you (for instance) see a clear picture over someone, instead of simply sharing what you see, try asking the Lord what it means. **The meaning is what will shape them, and that is where the prophetic skill set can truly shine.** As you release something that is clear, you create room for the Father's heart to minister to them.

As you do this, you can use the checks above to do your best to keep what you share on track and honoring to God.

And as you receive prophecy or help others process prophetic words, you now have a framework to which you can turn in order to assess what is shared with you.

APPLICATION: WHAT TO DO WITH A PROPHECY

W e were in the early days of helping our church (at the time) to transition into acceptance and practice of a naturally supernatural culture. Public prayer ministry was still a new experience for many, and so we were treading carefully so as to build support for a major shift in theology and practice.

One Sunday morning it felt right to offer a chance to come and kneel before the cross in response to the sermon (on giving everything to Jesus). We then invited our prayer ministry team to come and gently pray over those who were encountering God.

I (Alex) was especially led to a couple who were lying face down together, in quiet yet intense submission to God. As I knelt by them and prayed, I felt God give me a clear yet difficult word. Although I didn't know much about them or their life, I saw their hearts being broken, even shattered, but Jesus was there with His hands gently cupped around their hearts, holding them together and then mending all those breaks. I was reminded of the Japanese art of Kintsugi, which mends broken pottery using silver or gold as the 'glue', so that afterwards you can still see the history of the piece even though it has been fully mended. The thinking is that what results is more beautiful than the original. I had no idea what this could mean for them, but after the usual qualifications that this could just be me, I moved on and left them praying.

About a month later I went into a senior staff meeting to hear that this couple had just lost their young adult son to a drug overdose. The senior pastor of the church said he'd been round to visit them earlier (he knew them well), and within 10 minutes they'd told them about this word I'd shared with them. He admitted to the team that on the inside he'd thought, 'What has Alex gone and done now?! I'm going to kill him!' — but they had a completely different response. The moment they'd heard the word back on that Sunday, they knew it was about their son. Obviously they had prayed and reached out to him in multiple ways, but at one level his death, while devastating, was not a surprise.

In that moment of the deepest of grief, they received that picture as a word of comfort and a sign of the Father's compassionate love over their whole family, including their son.

As time went by, this couple were able to turn the loss of their son into an active and significant charity, which raised money via WWE-style wrestling bouts (their son's sport) to use in drug education campaigns in schools. Many months later they reminded me of that Sunday and the prophecy (it is a word which, needless to say, I recalled clearly), and how it had been such a support for them in the months that followed, and additionally as they allowed the Lord Jesus to 'kintsugi' their hearts back towards wholeness, particularly through their fundraising charity.

The other significant, though broader, impact of that word was that it authenticated prophetic ministry to many of the key leaders in the church, not through abstract teaching but as a result of very clear modeling of how it can bring profound comfort, even in the darkest of places.

HOW TO APPLY A PROPHECY

While most prophecies that you receive will be nothing as weighty as in the story above, when you do receive a prophecy and you are clear what it means, the next step is to ask God what to do with it, and when.

While Jesus is infinitely creative, here are ten of the most common ways you can apply a prophecy out of a heart of faith and patient trust.

1. ENCOURAGEMENT, COMFORT AND STRENGTHENING

It brings you general strengthening, encouragement or comfort. In our experience, this is perhaps the most common application - which should not be surprising in light of 1 Corinthians 14:3, *"But the one who prophesies speaks to people for their strengthening, encouraging and comfort."*

There is something hugely upbuilding when you sense the Lord's voice as you read the Bible, or worship, or sit in His presence, or when someone shares a prophetic word they have for you. Allow yourself to be encouraged - don't disdain that, for it is no small thing.

Consider: Is God simply wanting to bring encouragement?

2. PRAYER

It could be that the prophecy is for you to pray about and not to share any further. The Lord is revealing His heart and desire in some specific area of life, and you can pray into that topic with greater clarity, boldness and faith.

"Let us then approach God's throne of grace with confidence, so that we may receive mercy and find grace to help us in our time of need," reminds Hebrews 4:16. Prophetic insight is one of the ways that we can have greater confidence in drawing close to His throne of grace in prayer.

Consider: How should I/we pray differently?

3. IDENTITY AND DESTINY

Often a prophetic word helps to reveal or confirm someone's identity in Christ, and to release them further into their God-ordained destiny.

Paul declares in Ephesians 2:10, *"For we are God's handiwork, created in Christ Jesus to do good works, which God prepared in advance for us to do."*

The Lord loves to help us understand who we are created and crafted to be and become, and to grasp the calling and opportunities that He has set before us. Prophecy can be a powerful way for us to receive confirmation and guidance along the way. We have had many times where we've sensed something in our spirits about a change, and then we will receive a prophetic word which brings a confirmation via someone who has no idea what we have been thinking. In other seasons we've received prophetic words to persevere in a challenging situation, as the journey is part of the Lord's shaping of us for the future.

Consider: How do I now better understand my identity and/or destiny in Christ?

. . .

4. DIRECTION

All of us have times when we are making significant decisions about future steps. These could be for ourselves and our family, or perhaps in the area of work and career, or ministry, or in some other area of life.

"Whether you turn to the right or to the left, your ears will hear a voice behind you, saying, 'This is the way; walk in it.'" (Isaiah 30:21)

God loves to help steer us, and prophetic words are a key part of how He does this. They might bring a chink of light for the future hope, or a next step strategy to step into, or even a specific tactic for today's agenda.

Obviously you need to be wise here - we would strongly suggest not making huge decisions purely based off one prophecy from another person - but you can ask the Lord for confirmation from other sources when you find yourself in such a moment. Nevertheless, prophecy done right can indeed help with direction.

I (Hannah) had this experience a number of years ago when the Lord spoke to me directly about a specific church and city, and said that we would be moving there as a family. I felt it right to simply write down the word and pray into it, but didn't say anything to anyone else (including Alex), so as to allow the Lord to bring it about if it was from Him. Three long months later Alex was invited to join that church, much to his surprise! After we had individually prayed and fasted about the opportunity, I asked Alex to speak his thoughts first, and he said that he felt we should pursue this opportunity.

Only then did I share the word from three months prior. That in turn served as confirmation and encouragement about direction, both in the moment and also in the time that followed, as the move itself did not turn out to be as good as we had hoped, and naturally we wondered if we had heard wrong. Being able to come back to this preemptive revelation gave us the confidence to persevere in a very tough situation.

Consider: How does this feed into directional decisions for my life?

5. TEACHING

"I have not departed from your laws, for you yourself have taught me." (Psalm 119:102)

Sometimes God gives us a prophecy in order to teach us something. This will tend to be something specific about our own situation and walk with Him, but it is still vital to pay attention.

Katie is a friend of ours who was in a season where she was trying to go further into giving her all to God. One day she felt the Spirit tell her not to eat chicken anymore, and she agreed to do this... until the day she was at a big party and the main food there was one of her favorites - slow marinated BBQ chicken! Figuring that it would be okay, she put three or four strips of tasty chicken on her plate, choosing to ignore the still small voice reminding her of her commitment. As she took her first bite, it tasted absolutely terrible! Looking around the room she saw everyone else eating it happily, and realized that this wasn't a food poisoning situation. So Katie slid the chicken over onto her husband's plate, and stuck with salad. When we asked her why she thought this took place, she said it was simple: God loves obedience, which is central to walking deeply with Him.

Consider: What does Jesus want me to learn?

. . .

6. COUNSELING

God might give a prophetic word in order to unearth an issue for which you then seek additional prayer ministry or counseling. We believe that this is part of His shepherding of us, bringing His healing balm through the prayers and wise counsel of others, so that we might walk in wholeness.

"Carry each other's burdens, and in this way you will fulfill the law of Christ." (Galatians 6:2)

Because we tend to run from such things, a prophetic word might be what brings something to our attention, giving us faith to step into the help that we need.

Consider: Can I see something specific for which counseling/ prayer ministry would be helpful?

7. EVANGELISM

"Come, see a man who told me everything I ever did. Could this be the Messiah?" (John 4:29)

A prophecy might be for someone who is lost, bringing them closer to, or even fully into, the Kingdom of God. A great example of this is in John 4, where Jesus has clear prophetic insight into the heart and life of the Samaritan woman, which ends with not only her coming to faith, but also revival breaking out in the town.

"Many of the Samaritans from that town believed in him because of the woman's testimony, 'He told me everything I ever did.'" (John 4:39)

We have had the joy of seeing a close friend become a Christian after we shared a very clear and specific prophecy with her, where the Father spoke to her about His view of her identity. Obviously wisdom is required on timing and language, but an accurate prophecy can be the tipping point into salvation!

Consider: What is my next step in helping the recipient draw closer to salvation?

8. CORRECTION

We know from Hebrews 12:6 that, *"The Lord disciplines the one he loves, and he chastens everyone he accepts as his son."* Therefore it is not a surprise that sometimes a prophetic word is clearly a correction, or perhaps a warning, from the Lord.

This requires humility on the path of the recipient, in order to respond out of faith and not condemnation.

Earlier we said that we don't allow those we lead to bring correction via prophecy unless they have a very strong track record, and even then it is best done with a pastoral leader present. This is not because we don't think God corrects through prophecy (He clearly does), but because there is so much room for pastoral chaos until there is prophetic maturity.

However, sometimes the person sharing has zero idea that the prophecy is a correction or warning, or it could be that God speaks to your heart directly about something He wishes to correct in you.

Consider: Is there something for which I need to repent? And how should I live differently thereafter?

9. SPIRITUAL WARFARE

Spiritual warfare might be revealed through a prophecy, so that we are better placed to understand what is happening around us. It is easy for even the most seasoned Christian to become so caught up in their immediate situation that they forget to consider the spiritual dynamics that could be at play. Prophetic insight might bring that clarity, revealing the spiritual forces at work in a situation.

Ephesians 6:12 tells us that, *"Our struggle is not against flesh and blood…"*

This is a reminder that God can speak into our lives directly, to show what is going on in the spiritual realms and what the enemy is up to. He can show us how to avoid the enemy's traps, and also advance against him and his wily schemes.

Consider: If the enemy is at work, how should I pray and do spiritual battle?

10. Worship

Finally, a prophetic word may simply be there to bring us to our knees in worship and adoration. We hear it and are so blessed that we simply can't help but worship and honor our loving heavenly Father for His goodness and care.

"Let the message of Christ dwell among you richly as you teach and admonish one another with all wisdom through psalms, hymns, and songs from the Spirit, singing to God with gratitude in your hearts." (Colossians 3:16)

Consider: What about this prophecy makes me hungry to worship Jesus?

KEEP FLEXIBLE

Application is such a key part of the process of hearing God's voice. After all, there is no point in simply hearing Jesus and not putting what He reveals into action - that is the way to a life that is built on sand!

Of course, application is not necessarily a static thing - God can continue to speak in fresh ways through a significant prophecy. It is a good discipline to go back over the prophetic words from your past, as sometimes the Lord will bring fresh insight and revelation of their applicability into your life today.

PART II

NEXT STEPS

Having focused up to now on giving you teaching and content, this second section gives you lots of ways to put what you are reading and learning into practice.

This will come to you in 8 parts... along with an extra bonus at the very end!

1. Activation Exercises - Some simple exercises, which you can do solo and with others, to help train you in hearing God's voice.

2. Common Questions and Objections - We give you 1-2 sentence headline answers to some of the common questions that may have yourself and you'll probably be asked as you train others on this topic.

3. Incorporating Prophecy Into Church Life - Some initial thoughts on how to see your church flow in the prophetic.

4. Group Study Guide - Many of you will be using this book in a group setting, so here you'll find a guide to help stir up your conversation and next steps!

5. Scriptures to Ponder - While learning to hear God's voice might feel new and unusual to some, it is deeply anchored in the Bible. Here we simply list some of the key verses that have most shaped our thinking - and invite you to consider them for yourself, as you ask the Lord how He wants you to live them out today.

6. Further Reading - For those who like to read, here are some suggestions to help you along.

7. Prayer to Grow in Hearing God's Voice - This is a longer, written-out prayer that you might like to use to express your desire to hear God's voice more clearly.

8. And Finally - We share how you can connect with us, access more of our free and paid for resources, and continue to step further into a naturally supernatural lifestyle.

7

ACTIVATION EXERCISES

NEXT STEPS 1

I n order to move further into hearing God's voice and being able to prophesy, it is important to practice.

Like any gift from God, He does not simply plop prophecy fully formed into your lap! Instead, it is something into which you must choose to grow. This requires you to dig deeper into Scripture to understand how the gift works, to learn good practice from those who are more experienced, and then recognize how it connects with the unique combination of your personality, story, and context.

Just as an athlete practices a sport and does warm up exercises first, or a musician practices an instrument with routine scales, so spiritually, by doing some fairly artificial exercises, we can practice and become better attuned to the voice of God. This in turn helps us to be ready when the needed moment of revelation and Kingdom breakthrough arises.

This requires discipline and experimentation in environments where you can make mistakes and learn, without causing ongoing pastoral damage to others. Walking this journey in community is vital.

Some of that wisdom will come from the wider church and some from your local church. While we as authors can be one of the many voices who enable you to access the wider church's understanding and experience of the prophetic gifts, we cannot help you be accountable in your specific situation. For that, you need people who can look you in the eye and help you grow, in a spirit of love, encouragement, and accountability.

To move you along in that process, here are some activation exercises. You will see that they come in three contexts: things you can do individually, some you can do in pairs, and others to be done in a group context. Obviously, these are jumping off points, so please do adapt them as you wish.

Bear in mind that, because these are artificial constructs, they might feel a bit odd to do! The goal is to stretch you in hearing God's voice, giving you greater confidence that you are indeed hearing Him.

INDIVIDUALLY

1. Ask God to speak to you personally through the Bible. Turn to the Psalms and read until you sense a phrase, verse or passage that resonates with you in a deeper way. Write down what you sense (even if you aren't sure or it feels a bit simple!).

Then take a few minutes to pray and start to weigh what you heard.

If possible, share with another Christian and gain from their insight.

2. Put on a worship song. As you listen, ask God to reveal to you what He thinks of you. Recognize that for most of us the temptation will be to process this solely through our cognitive reasoning - which is not the best filter for receiving words of love and affirmation! Simply enjoy the experience, and weigh later on what you sense.

IN PAIRS

3. *Ask God for a picture of an animal that represents the person you are with, and why that is the case.* What is God saying through that? Share with your partner, and weigh it together.

4. *In pairs, ask God what color is associated with your partner, and why.* Share the insights with each other.

AS A GROUP

5. *Tell the group that you are going to ask God to reveal Himself in a tangible physical way to each person.* Encourage them to be attentive to what they are sensing - it could be a sense of peace, a temperature change, a sensation or tingling in part of their body, a weight or lightness, a change in their breathing, etc. The goal is then to engage with the Lord, and allow Him to speak either through that physical sensation or, now that He has someone's attention, to speak about something else. After explaining, invite people to be still before God, probably closing their eyes as you pray and then as you all wait on God.

6. *Tray exercise* - Either do a quick image search online for 'tray of objects', or create your own tray of varied and interesting items.

Ideally have the tray covered until you have explained the exercise - you might remember doing this as a memorization game as a child! However, in this case you are not memorizing, but instead asking the Holy Spirit to highlight one of the objects, and to reveal to you why. For instance, He might speak about your place of mission through a pattern on an object on the tray.

Give the group 5 minutes to look at the tray, and then ask for a few people to feedback about their experience of the exercise. Bear in mind that some might not want to share in the group if it was a more personal revelation, so you don't need everyone to speak.

8

COMMON QUESTIONS AND OBJECTIONS

NEXT STEPS 2

Think of this section as a quick-fire round, where we try to give headline answers to questions that are often asked on this topic. The aim here is to remind you of the key points, most of which are unpacked in fuller depth in the main chapters.

GENERAL

Is hearing God's voice in the Bible?

Yes - Jesus makes clear that His disciples are the ones who hear what He says and then respond in obedience. The book of Acts is full of examples of people in the early church having a wide range of prophetic revelations, and Paul teaches at length about how to do this in wise and Kingdom-building ways.

How do we stop it undermining the value of the Bible?

The primary way God speaks to us is through the Scriptures, and the first test of any prophecy is whether it is in accord with the Bible. Good prophetic ministry only enhances our value for the written Word. The Bible is God speaking to all people in all places at all times, whereas prophecy is for a specific person/people in a specific place at a specific time.

CAN ANYONE DO IT?

If you are committed to Christ as Savior and Lord, then yes, you definitely can (and should) hear God's voice as He leads you through your life. In fact, of all the gifts of the Spirit, Paul chooses to instruct us to especially desire that we might prophesy (1 Corinthians 14:1) - presumably not to frustrate us, but because it is open to, and is vital for, all disciples of Jesus.

IS PROPHESYING TO BE DONE OVER THE CHURCH CORPORATELY, OR WITH INDIVIDUALS?

Both can and should occur.

Wisdom would suggest that the safer place to practice is in smaller settings, since the feedback will be quicker and less awkward. We have found small groups and missional communities to be excellent contexts to grow in these gifts, although prophecy can also be a healthy part of weekend public services.

REVELATION

WHAT ARE SOME OF THE DIFFERENT WAYS WE CAN HEAR GOD'S VOICE?

We see four main ways that cover 90% of revelation: the Bible, seeing stuff, hearing stuff, and knowing stuff. We unpack these (and list some other ways God reveals things) in Chapter 3 on Revelation.

How does revelation become more natural?

It takes time to learn how to recognize God's voice and promptings above the clutter of everything going on around and within us.

However, with practice, you can learn how to almost instantly tune in to what He is revealing in a situation, so our best advice is to seize every opportunity to draw closer to Jesus and to quietly listen to the still small voice (or images and thoughts) of His inner prompting.

How do I unclutter my mind?

Christian meditation is distinctive from that practiced by other religions in that we do not seek to empty our minds, but rather we fill them with Christ. This results in us being more deeply focused upon Him and His glory. The same principle applies to hearing God's voice: we don't seek so much to empty our minds, but rather we come into His presence with thanksgiving and praise, we read His Word, and we worship Him. As we wait in that place the revelation will come, and we receive *"the deep things of God"* (1 Corinthians 2:10) - even if that is simply a reminder of His goodness and awesome beauty.

INTERPRETATION

How do I discern what is from God and what is from the enemy?

We would suggest six questions to help you weigh a

prophecy: Does it line up with the Bible? Does it reflect God's heart of love? Does the speaker have an agenda? Do other wise people think it's from God? Does it resonate? Does it prove true?

How do I get over the fear of being wrong?

In contrast to the Old Testament, the New Testament shifts the emphasis away from the speaker being 100% correct and onto the listener(s) to weigh and evaluate what has been shared (we write more about this in our book *Operating in Words of Knowledge and Wisdom*). This means you WILL sometimes be wrong when you share something you think might be from God, since like all of the other gifts of the Spirit, prophecy doesn't simply appear into your life fully-formed and with zero need for development and maturing.

What do we do when we get it wrong?

It is vital to have a heart that is submitted to leadership, actively welcomes feedback and accountability, and always shares with humility. In a safe environment, you can process what did and didn't work (including how you shared), apologize where necessary, and keep learning and growing.

APPLICATION

What do I do with a big prophecy?

If you receive a word that feels especially significant, we would suggest that you write it down, pray over it for a number of days, ask God to help you weigh what is from Him, and discern how He wants you to respond. You should also draw in other spiritually mature voices in your life, and seek confirmation from other unrelated places if you are going to make significant life changes as a result.

How does this tie into prayer?

A prophetic word is never meant to be a replacement for personal prayer — in fact, it should drive you even more to your knees! One of the most common applications from a prophecy is prayer, as Jesus gives you a specific topic to wrestle through with Him.

Is there only one application from each prophetic word?

We find that often there are multiple applications, or next steps, that we can take when we receive a prophetic word. Clearly prayer is pretty much a no-brainer, and God's prophetic words will bring encouragement, strengthening, and comfort. We might also be led into greater spiritual warfare, or evangelistic impulse, or perhaps we sense the Lord's leading for our direction as we gain greater clarity on our calling. And you might find that you look back over prophetic words after some time and see, with the benefit of hindsight, how much more truth there was in the given word than you first realized.

We are designed
for a familiarity
with God that is
both intimate
and reverent.

9

INCORPORATING PROPHECY INTO CHURCH LIFE

NEXT STEPS 3

I n each of our books in the Naturally Supernatural series, we like to offer some suggestions for how to incorporate what you're learning into the life of your church. This includes thinking about weekend services, group life, how leadership works, and your witness to the wider community.

For the prophetic gifts, we have written an entire book on this - *Building a Prophetic Culture* - since there is way more ground to cover than will fit into an appendix, or even an additional chapter or two!

In advance of you reading that (which we hope you will!), here are a couple of quick thoughts:

1. KEEP PURSUING THIS PERSONALLY.

Ask God to help you have more opportunities to step into these gifts, as you reflect on your experiences through the lens of Scripture. We would encourage you to use the activation exercises and steps we have shared to help you grow. The naturally supernatural lifestyle is as much caught as taught, so as you model this and move in the prophetic with greater ease, others will see its power and impact and will copy what you are doing.

2. Actively seek out accountability.

Unaccountable prophetic voices are unbiblical, dangerous to the church, and undermining of our witness for Christ. Even if you find yourself in a church community that is not experienced in the more supernatural gifts, there will still be godly men and women there who can help you discern, process, and keep growing in healthy ways. Pray and ask God to give you these discerning friends.

"Those who disregard discipline despise themselves, but the one who heeds correction gains understanding." (Proverbs 15:32)

3. Ensure that your personal devotion to Christ is deepening.

Ultimately any prophetic ministry flows out of our walk as disciple-making disciples of Jesus. This means that in every area of life we commit to being ones who hear and obey what He is saying. There are already multiple areas in our lives where what Jesus has revealed about His will is a huge stretch for us (re-read the Sermon on the Mount, for example!), so keep pursuing those things. The prophetic gifts rest the most meaningfully on a person who is overflowing with the love of Jesus.

10

GROUP STUDY GUIDE

NEXT STEPS 4

F or groups wishing to study this book together, here are some questions to help move your conversation in a productive direction. We recommend that you read the relevant chapter(s) in advance of your discussion. Make sure you do the activation exercises, to ensure that you combine both reasoning and practice in your exploration. The list of Scriptures to ponder (Next Steps 5) will also be useful in your conversations.

Chapter 1 — Our Hearing Problem

- What most excites you about the potential of hearing God more clearly?
- For you personally, what are the top two or three things that most drown out God's voice?
- What helps you quiet your spirit to listen to God better?
- What fears or concerns do you have about the prophetic gifts being used more openly and fully?
- Do the prayer exercise at the end of the chapter.

CHAPTER 2 — DEFINING PROPHECY

- Which of the definitions of prophecy in the chapter most resonated with you?
- When have you or a family member ever experienced the love of God through prophecy?
- On a scale of 1 to 5, how eagerly do you desire that you might prophesy? Explain your choice of number.
- As you look at the examples from Jesus and the Early Church prophesying, how does that compare to your church? Is their example a fair expectation?
- Do the goal exercise at the end of the chapter.

CHAPTER 3 — REVELATION: HOW GOD SPEAKS

- Do you have any concerns about becoming over-mystical and strange as you grow in the prophetic gifts? How can you overcome them?
- How would you answer the cautious Christian who says that since we have the Bible we don't need prophecy?
- Of the list of the 12 main ways God releases revelation, which ones have you experienced?
- As you look again at the list, name one area that you would like to grow in. What would be a specific goal to set to achieve this?
- In 'Next Steps 1: Activation Exercises,' do exercise 6 (with the tray of objects).

CHAPTER 4 — HOW TO SHARE REVELATION

- What helps you self-assess if a revelation is from God or not?
- In your church/ group, do you have a 'No dates, no mates, no direction, no correction' type of rule for

prophesying? Even if prophecy is new to you, why might it be a wise idea to adopt that rule?

- Have you ever heard prophecy done with weird or old fashioned language? How did it make you feel? What sort of language do you want to make normal in your group/ church?
- Have you ever been prophesied over? How did it feel? What was helpful, and what was unhelpful, in the way that you experienced it?
- In 'Next Steps 1: Activation Exercises,' do exercise 3 (animal name).

CHAPTER 5 — INTERPRETATION: HOW TO TEST A PROPHECY

- What was your reaction to Alex's story of being proposed to? Can God tell someone who they're to marry?
- What do you find helpful about the analogy of the Bible as the Rosetta Stone for interpreting revelation from God?
- Who would you ask for wisdom in weighing a very meaningful prophetic word?
- What should we do with a prophecy that doesn't prove to be true?
- Have you ever had a dream that was spiritual in origin? How did you interpret it?
- In 'Next Steps 1: Activation Exercises,' do exercise 4 (color).

CHAPTER 6 — APPLICATION: WHAT TO DO WITH A PROPHECY

- When God reveals something to you, how good are you at sensing His timing and expectations of you to act?
- If God revealed something incredible and gossip-

worthy about a friend of yours, but made clear that
this revelation was only to help you pray for them,
how easy would you find it to not say anything to
them (or anyone else) over a long period of time?

- Have you ever seen prophecy shared with a person
who isn't a Christian? How do you think an accurate
prophetic word might impact some of your neighbors
or colleagues who are far from God?

- When have you sensed the Spirit pinpointing
something in you about which He wants you to
confess and repent? How did that feel?

- Why do you think prophecy often stirs up spiritual
battle?

- In 'Next Steps 1: Activation Exercises,' do exercise 5
(tangible revelation).

11

SCRIPTURES TO PONDER

NEXT STEPS 5

We have tried to root this book strongly in the Bible, since we believe that the naturally supernatural lifestyle is one that is commanded, commended, and demonstrated there. As theology is built, it must be shaped by Scripture.

However, we also recognize that no one is fully correct in their interpretation of Scripture since we all bring our preferences, blind spots, history, and culture into how we read it. So to help level the playing field a little, here are some texts that we have found particularly helpful in growing in the prophetic gifts. These are beneficial to read, to study in context, and even to memorize, so that your theology and practice can be allied as closely as possible to the Bible's universal revelation to all people at all times and in all places.

"Would that all the Lord's people were prophets, that the Lord would put His Spirit upon them!" (Numbers 11:29)

"*The Lord said, 'Go out and stand on the mountain in the presence of the Lord, for the Lord is about to pass by.' Then a great and powerful wind tore the mountains apart and shattered the rocks before the Lord, but the Lord was not in the wind. After the wind there was an earthquake, but the Lord was not in the earthquake. After the earthquake came a fire, but the Lord was not in the fire. And after the fire came a gentle whisper.*" (1 Kings 19:11-12)

"*I will instruct you and teach you in the way you should go; I will counsel you with my loving eye on you. Do not be like the horse or the mule, which have no understanding but must be controlled by bit and bridle or they will not come to you.*" (Psalm 32:8-9)

"*Be still and know that I am God.*" (Psalm 46:1)

"*Call to me and I will answer you and tell you great and unsearchable things you do not know.*" (Jeremiah 33:3)

"*And afterward, I will pour out My Spirit on all people. Your sons and daughters will prophesy, your old men will dream dreams, your young men will see visions.*" (Joel 2:28)

"*Jesus answered, 'I tell you, Peter, before the rooster crows today, you will deny three times that you know me'.*" (Luke 22:34)

"*Jesus said to her, 'You are right when you say you have no husband. The fact is, you have had five husbands, and the man you now have is not your husband'.*" (John 4:17-18)

Jesus: "*The Son can do nothing by himself; he can do only what he sees his Father doing, because whatever the Father does the Son also does.*" (John 5:19)

Jesus: "*My sheep listen to my voice; I know them, and they follow me.*" (John 10:27)

Jesus: "*For I did not speak on my own, but the Father who sent me commanded me to say all that I have spoken.*" (John 12:49)

"*One of them, named Agabus, stood up and through the Spirit* predicted that a severe famine would spread over the entire Roman world. (This happened during the reign of Claudius.)" (Acts 11:28)

"In Lystra there sat a man who was lame. He had been that way from birth and had never walked. He listened to Paul as he was speaking. Paul looked directly at him, saw that he had faith to be healed and called out, 'Stand up on your feet!' At that, the man jumped up and began to walk." (Acts 14:8-10)

"During the night Paul had a vision of a man of Macedonia standing and begging him, 'Come over to Macedonia and help us'." (Acts 16:9)

"So faith comes from hearing, and hearing through the word of Christ." (Romans 10:17 ESV)

"If I have the gift of prophecy and can fathom all mysteries and all knowledge… but do not have love, I am nothing." (1 Corinthians 13:2)

"Follow the way of love and eagerly desire gifts of the Spirit, especially prophecy." (1 Corinthians 14:1)

"The one who prophesies speaks to people for their strengthening, encouraging and comfort." (1 Corinthians 14:3)

"Two or three prophets should speak, and the others should weigh carefully what is said." (1 Corinthians 14:29)

"The spirits of prophets are subject to the control of prophets." (1 Corinthians 14:32)

"I keep asking that the God of our Lord Jesus Christ, the glorious Father, may give you the Spirit of wisdom and revelation, so that you may know him better." (Ephesians 1:17)

"Do not quench the Spirit. Do not treat prophecies with contempt but test them all; hold on to what is good, reject every kind of evil." (1 Thessalonians 5:19-22)

"We have confidence to enter the Most Holy Place by the blood of Jesus." (Hebrews 10:19)

"Whoever has ears, let them hear what the Spirit says to the churches." (Revelation 3:22)

12

FURTHER READING

NEXT STEPS 6

O ver the years we have read many books on growing in the naturally supernatural. Our aim here is to give you a list that is not overwhelming, yet does have a good mixture of books to help you develop in this area. We have not included books that are out of print or hard to source in the United States.

As you know, this book is part of a series, and initially we envisioned a unique reading list for each individual book. However, many authors cover a variety of topics in their work, and so it seemed simpler to create one master list for the entire series, which we might tweak a little from time to time.

———

These are in author alphabetical order, with a comment or two to introduce each book to you.

- **Ruth Haley Barton, *Invitation to Solitude and Silence* (2004)** — One woman's journey into the necessity of regular times of withdrawing to be with

Jesus. Each chapter ends with a practice or exercise to try out, which gives the book a healthy focus on application.

- **Mike Bickle, *Growing in the Prophetic* (1995)** — From someone who pastored a church with a prominent and yet at times chaotic prophetic ministry, those lessons learned create an insightful and practical resource.

- **Christoph Blumhardt, *The Gospel of God's Reign* (2014)** — 19th Century German theologian, also a prominent evangelist, faith healer, and politician, his writings focus on bringing God's Kingdom around us by all means possible. Stimulating, even if you don't agree with everything he says!

- **Shawn Bolz, *God Secrets* (2017)** — Engaging teaching on developing the gift of words of knowledge, including content on what to do when you get it wrong. Shawn Bolz has a very public track record of operating in this gift, and does a good job demystifying its usage.

- **Shawn Bolz, *Translating God* (2015)** — A down-to-earth yet inspiring read that focuses on training people in how to step into the prophetic gifts, with some great stories, a high level of transparency from the author, and teaching that is so practical.

- **Michael Cassidy, *Bursting the Wineskins* (1983)** — Written from an African perspective by the man who is the Honorary Chair of the Lausanne Movement, Michael uses his story as a framework to teach Biblically about entering into life in the Spirit.

- **Dave Clayton,** *Revival Starts Here: A Short Conversation on Prayer, Fasting and Revival for Beginners Like Me* **(2018)** — Practical and non-guilt inducing challenge to step more into fasting and prayer, with lots of application ideas. A great short read!

- **Jack Deere,** *Surprised by the Power of the Spirit* **(1993)** — The inspiring story of how a cessationist seminary professor had his life and ministry turned upside down as he experienced the power and presence of the Holy Spirit.

- **Gordon Fee,** *God's Empowering Presence* **(1994)** — Fee was one of the first Pentecostals to earn a PhD in Biblical studies, and he combines the two streams in this book by literally exegeting every reference to the Spirit in Paul's writings - but the result is anything but a dry academic read.

- **Bill Johnson,** *God is Good* **(2016)** — An uplifting read about trusting in the goodness of God as revealed in Scripture, so that we in turn can reveal His goodness in the power of the Spirit to a broken world.

- **Bill Johnson & Randy Clark,** *The Essential Guide to Healing* **(2011)** — An excellent book on how to heal the sick, with practical teaching, stirring stories, and sensible wisdom for developing this ministry in a church context.

- **Charles Kraft, *Defeating Dark Angels* (2016)** — Clear, Biblically grounded teaching on how demonic oppression takes place, and how to minister deliverance. Kraft has many books, and we found this one to be very helpful and practical.

- **George Eldon Ladd, *The Gospel of the Kingdom* (1959)** — A hugely influential book, which explores the mystery that the Kingdom of God is both now and simultaneously not yet, and how the Spirit empowers us to go out on mission to extend God's kingly rule.

- **Francis MacNutt, *Healing* (1974 - although look for the updated version)** — This was the first modern-era book on healing that has (deservedly) been widely read, and you can see its influence still today. Very practical and packed full of nuggets of wisdom.

- **Charles Price, *The Real Faith* (1930s)** — After experiencing baptism in the Spirit in the 1920s, his ministry was transformed and saw incredible healings. This short book is the best reflection on the nature of faith and the naturally supernatural life that we have found.

- **Derek Prince, *They Shall Expel Demons* (1998)** — Prince wrote numerous books on deliverance, and this is an excellent primer into this area. Sensible, Biblical, faith-filled, it contains wise teaching and helpful stories gained from many years of experience.

- **David Pytches, *Come Holy Spirit* (1994)** — Written more like a logical, logistical, list-driven handbook, this was such a help in our early years of ministering in the power of the Spirit, as it gives you all the major points in a systematic way.

- **Jon Ruthven,** *On the Cessation of the Charismata: The Protestant Polemic on Postbiblical Miracles* **(1993)** — A brilliant deconstruction of cessationism, written from a scholarly Biblical perspective, full of close exegesis of texts and clear arguments.

- **Jordan Seng,** *Miracle Work* **(2012)** — A great overview of ministering in the spiritual gifts, with each teaching chapter followed by a short story chapter, which makes it all feel very grounded and attainable.

- **Sam Storms,** *Practicing the Power* **(2017)** — If you come from a Reformed Calvinist perspective, Sam does a great job of showing how stepping into the spiritual gifts is deeply rooted in Scripture.

- **Jerry Trousdale,** *Miraculous Movements: How Hundreds of Thousands of Muslims Are Falling in Love with Jesus* **(2012)** — We both love this book! It is packed full of inspirational stories of how the church is growing globally AND gives tools that we can use here in the West.

- **Jerry Trousdale & Glenn Sunshine,** *The Kingdom Unleashed* **(2018)** - Revealing insights on how the church in the Global South is growing rapidly through Disciple-Making Movements. Lots of takeaways on living the principles of Acts today.

- **Kris Vallotton,** *Basic Training for the Prophetic Ministry* **(2014)** — A down-to-earth, clear and helpful training in the prophetic gifts, which feels as if a very fatherly member of your church is steering you into greater maturity!

- **Mark & Pam Virkler,** *How to Hear God's Voice* **(2005)** — Designed more as a workbook (with lots of note taking space), it contains Biblical teaching and helpful exercises, and in particular a focus on encountering God through waiting on Him.

- **David & Paul Watson,** *Contagious Disciple Making* **(2014)** — Learning from Disciple-Making Movements across the globe, the stories here are fabulous, and there is much content on how to make disciples in a naturally supernatural way.

- **Dallas Willard,** *The Divine Conspiracy* **(1998)** — An engaging and thoughtful study about the nature of the Gospel of the Kingdom that Jesus preaches - which is not a set of rules to follow, but a declaration of God's active rule and His invitation for us to enter in and partner with Him.

- **John Wimber & Kevin Springer,** *Power Evangelism* **(1985)** — Explains Jesus' theology of the Kingdom, and then moves to show how this transforms our evangelism, with lots of practical stories and ideas for taking your next step.

- **John Wimber & Kevin Springer,** *Power Healing* **(1987)** — A classic text that has influenced many leaders. It creates a Biblical theology of healing, based on how Jesus operated, and then applies those principles with wisdom and experience.

- **Brother Yun, *The Heavenly Man* (2002)** — An inspirational first-hand account from Chinese house church leader Brother Yun, who has led a huge movement in the power of the Spirit in the face of severe persecution. Some amazing stories!

As disciples of Jesus, we need to be people who operate in the power and authority of the Holy Spirit.

13

PRAYER TO GROW IN HEARING GOD'S VOICE

NEXT STEPS 7

F ather, thank You for the wonderful gifts of Your Spirit! I eagerly desire them, especially that I might prophesy.

May I hear the gentle whispers of your Spirit of wisdom and revelation, so that I may know You better - and help others do the same. Tune my ear to listen to Your voice. Graciously teach me to discern the truths and mysteries that You desire to reveal, the great and unsearchable things that I do not know, so that I can better join You in advancing Your Kingdom purposes here on earth.

Your word says, *"If your gift is prophesying, then prophesy in accordance with your faith."* I humbly ask for a significant faith increase in me, especially in those situations where in the natural there might be little hope, but in the Spirit there is still so much possibility. May those prophetic revelations stir up great faith, hope, and love in others.

I recognize that it is easy to become distracted by fear, doubt, and the cares of this world, so I ask for the grace to keep my heart and mind locked onto You. When the enemy tries to draw me away, may I choose to be still, and again know that You are my God. Keep me humble in moments where the gift is clearly at work, so that the glory and my dependency remain upon You.

Thank You for the community of believers around me. Please raise up women and men from my church community who are also on this journey of learning to hear Your voice more clearly. Please give me people who can help me grow in the prophetic through accountability, encouragement, and a shared pursuit of the Lord Jesus Christ.

As I look to step further into prophetic gifts, may I only operate out of a heart of love. Please help me to lay down my agendas, and instead serve in ways that honor You and demonstrably value the people over whom I prophesy. May I minister out of a humble, submitted heart of compassion for others, and speak prophetic words that truly reflect Your great love, kindness, and goodness.

In Jesus' name I pray,

Amen.

14

CONNECT WITH US AND ACCESS MORE!

NEXT STEPS 8

F irstly, THANK YOU for taking the time to read this book! Our hope and prayer is that you now feel greater confidence in hearing God's voice, and that you can step further into a naturally supernatural lifestyle.

However, the key is not to stop now! If you would like to see your investment of time, energy, and prayer produce a far greater return, then you will need to keep practicing and learning. And we are here to help you on your journey...

ACCESS MORE RESOURCES

As a couple, our call from God is to equip the wider church with practical tools like this book. To help facilitate this, we lead the team at Dandelion Resourcing, which exists to empower Christians like you to go and form disciple-making disciples of Jesus in naturally supernatural ways.

With passionate believers like you in mind, we have developed a variety of resources:

- This book is part of *The Naturally Supernatural Series*,

each of which combines Biblical theology, field-tested step-by-step teaching, and repeatable personal practices. Topics we cover in the series include the prophetic gifts, healing, deliverance, building a Kingdom theology, being filled with the Holy Spirit, living a miraculous life, and becoming a naturally supernatural missionary. *As a gift from us to you, at the end of this book you will find a free sample of one of our other books, to build on what you have already been learning and implementing!*

- Every couple of weeks we release a new, FREE coaching video, which we would love for you to receive! These form part of an equipping series, where you can access practical training that you can use both personally and also to train your team or group. However, the catch is that each video comes with specific homework that we expect you to put into practice! The goal of these short (TED talk length) videos is to equip you to go into the world as naturally supernatural disciple-making missionaries. To watch the latest video — and access the extensive archive — please visit dandelionresourcing.com/blog.

- We offer more focused coaching, both individually and in small online groups, details of which are on our website - dandelionresourcing.com/what. There is also an option for church consulting, which Alex has done across the United States and in a number of other nations.

- If you would like one or both of us to preach or teach at your church, special event, or conference, we would be honored to hear from you! It doesn't need to be on naturally supernatural topics - we have lived, written, and spoken extensively on discipleship, missional living, marriage, and parenting. Please do reach out to us and we can have that conversation.

The best place to find out more is at our website, dandelionresourcing.com. There you can sign up for us to let you know whenever there is a new coaching video posted, or when a book or resource is released (roughly one email every couple of weeks - and you can easily unsubscribe at any time!)

SHARE YOUR FEEDBACK

If you have any questions or suggestions about the content of this book, please feel free to be in touch with either of us. If you go to dandelionresourcing.com, there is a 'Contact Us' form on the site.

We're also on social media at the following spots:

Instagram: instagram.com/alexabsalom

Facebook: facebook.com/dandelionresourcing

Twitter: twitter.com/AlexAbsalom

LinkedIn: linkedin.com/in/alexabsalom

COULD YOU HELP US OUT?

If you have enjoyed this book, would you mind doing us a quick favor?

The best way for others to find out about a resource like this is through personal recommendation (think about what makes you investigate a new book!). With that mind, we would be so honored *if you would take a moment to share a quick review with others.*

The #1 place is on Amazon - pop in your stars and write a comment, and that will help us enormously. (As you no doubt know, the more reviews, the more their algorithms will high-light this book to others.)

In addition, please do share about this book (post a photo of you holding the cover!) on social media — feel free to tag us in the shot!

Thank you so much in advance.

Again, thank you for reading - we're praying that you have so much Jesus-honoring fruitfulness as you step further into a naturally supernatural lifestyle.

With love and blessings,

Alex and Hannah

ACKNOWLEDGMENTS

Over the years so many people have helped us grow into a naturally supernatural lifestyle. Some have been leaders, others friends, and yet others would never know our name or faces, but have shaped us through their teachings, books, podcasts, and lives.

However, a number of specific people have intentionally helped us with this book — and we are thankful for each one of them! They include Caity Shinnick, whose creative and thoughtful cover design and internal layout work turned our chicken-scratch into a book with style and charm, Emily Berg for her eagle-eyed book editing, Amy Honeycutt and David Patterson for proof reading the far less glamorous early versions, and Alan Hirsch for the quotes that he loves to text Alex! We are also grateful for our Naturally Supernatural Coaching Cohorts, where we have together worked through a lot of this material, and from whom we continue to learn. Finally, a huge thank you to our friends who have prayed for us during this process, and cheered us on with words of faith, encouragement, and love.

Healings are not just proof of Jesus' message, they are elements of his actual message.

BONUS: FREE SAMPLE FROM OUR NEW BOOK

HEALING THE SICK

By Alex and Hannah Absalom

OUR DAUGHTER HAS HER LIFE BACK

In the early days of developing a culture of prayer for healing at our former church in Ohio, we began offering opportunities to receive healing prayer during most of the weekend worship services. One Sunday a young woman, who was back home from Boston visiting her parents, came forward and shared that she had stage 4 ovarian cancer. Her doctors had told her that they had run out of options for treatment, and could now only offer pain relief and short term delays.

Several of us gathered around and began prayer ministry, crying out to the Lord for complete healing. During that time, the young woman experienced the peace and presence of Jesus come upon her, and she left feeling refreshed and more deeply aware of His love. Over the next few days she felt increasingly energized, and at her next doctor's appointment, confusion reigned. It turned out that the cancer had completely disappeared from her body!

The doctors assumed this must be a strange remission, so followed her for many months, until eventually she was declared to be fully healthy. In her medical notes, the doctor recorded, "This is a miracle, for which I have no medical explanation."

Several years later, when our family moved on from Ohio to California, we received a lovely card from this young woman's parents. They shared that their daughter remained fully healthy, was completely cancer free, and that she was marrying her fiance the following month. They concluded with the simple words: "Our daughter has her life back, and we are all so incredibly grateful to God."

WHY DID JESUS HEAL?

Jesus came to definitively reveal the nature of the Father to us. In John 5:19 He said, *"Very truly I tell you, the Son can do nothing by himself; he can do only what he sees his Father doing, because whatever the Father does the Son also does."*

If Jesus reveals the nature of God the Father, and Jesus heals, then clearly healing is part of the Father's nature and will. We have a loving heavenly Father who hates sickness more than we do, and loves to see healing released into every part of His children's lives.

For Jesus, healing was a core part of His message and His ministry.

Jesus' very name, which means 'God saves', reveals so much about His identity and the purpose of His ministry. Since Biblical thought is holistic, salvation through Jesus means that He comes to save us in every sphere of existence. He is redeeming the whole of creation, including our physical bodies.

At the cross we discover that salvation impacts every aspect of our humanity. This means that healings are not just proof of Jesus' message, they are elements of His actual message. Healings don't merely demonstrate that Jesus can save us, but rather they are in themselves salvation breaking into the here and now.

Of course, Jesus' role as our Savior is about far more than physical healing, and humanity's greatest need is for our sins to be forgiven and our relationship with God to be fully restored. Yet what Jesus offers is not some disembodied escape from the physical world. He is interested in saving the whole you: spirit, body, mind, and emotions.

BUT WHAT IF...

At this point our minds tend to jump straight to thinking about all the "What Ifs" - "What if healing doesn't take place? What if they think it's their fault? What if the family members don't see their prayers answered? What if the illness is long-term? What if they end up dying from that sickness? What if they don't have enough faith? What if they aren't healed and walk away from Jesus?"

Those are all legitimate questions, which we will address later in this book. However, it is important not to build our theology on our fears and failures, since to do so requires us to subordinate Scripture to our experiences, which is never going to produce a gospel-centered worldview.

Instead, we must intentionally start with a clear-eyed under-standing of God's character and actions in relation to sickness and healing.

GOD, SICKNESS, AND HEALING

One of God's self-chosen names in Old Testament Hebrew is 'Jehovah Rapha', which in English is translated as 'the God who heals'. The word *rapha* means to restore, to heal, or to make healthy. He is the mighty God who loves to heal us - spirit, body, mind, and emotions.

God describes Himself as healer in Exodus 15:26, and throughout the Psalms there are cries for fresh healing, as well as thanksgivings for healings that have already taken place (e.g. Psalm 6:2 and 30:2). God is described as the Lord *"who forgives all your sins and heals all your diseases, who redeems your life from the pit and crowns you with love and compassion."* (Psalm 103:3-4)

In Isaiah and Jeremiah there are prophecies about a coming time when God's healings will occur more freely and fully (e.g. Isaiah 57:17-18, Jeremiah 30:17, and 33:6). And the classic text comes in Isaiah 53:5, which talks prophetically about the coming Messiah's saving role, which of course we see fulfilled in the work of Jesus: *"But he was pierced for our transgressions, he was crushed for our iniquities; the punishment that brought us peace was on him, and by his wounds we are healed."*

In the life and ministry of Jesus there are multiple occasions - almost too many to count - when He healed the sick. And He intentionally trained and commissioned His followers to do the same thing, sharing His power and authority to drive forward this expression of His active Kingdom rule. In another section in this book we list out many of these passages, along with examples from Acts, and teaching on healing from the letters.

But here is the point: Jesus actively sought to heal the sick. And for Him, it wasn't simply a kind thing to do, but rather it was a central aspect of His message.

JESUS' ATTITUDE TO SICKNESS

Throughout the Gospels, Jesus is consistently and repeatedly clear that sickness is an enemy of God and His people. There is not a single incidence of Him adopting a stoic attitude towards illness.

In Matthew 8:16-17, Jesus drove out the demonic spirits *"with a word"* and *"healed all the sick"*. Matthew then comments, *"This was to fulfill what was spoken through the prophet Isaiah: 'He took up our infirmities and bore our diseases'."*

Unlike some dreadful theologies today, we never catch Jesus saying something like, "Well, this sickness might be tough, but it's doing wonders for your character, so the Father says leave it in place for a little while longer." Likewise, He didn't respond to a request for healing by saying, "I wish I could help, but it's not your time for healing yet. The Father wants you to stick it out for longer."

Instead, Jesus always treated sickness as deeply and personally offensive, a violation of His good creation, and something to be fiercely opposed. It is interesting that every person who came to Jesus seeking to be made well experienced a complete healing - He never turned anyone down or away.

In Mark 1:41, a leper asked if Jesus would be willing to make him clean. The response is fascinating. Jesus was indignant that anyone could for even one moment think that He was not willing to bring deliverance and healing! Of course He wants us whole! He therefore touched the man and said, *"I am willing. Be clean."* The power and authority that Jesus carried meant that, when He touched the leper (who was regarded as deeply unclean by the society of the time), Jesus was not made unclean - instead, the unclean was made clean at His touch. Such is His transformative strength.

All this leads us to conclude that health and healing are the ordinary response of a loving Father to His children, and Jesus went out of His way to reveal the fullness of this truth.

Our book, *Healing the Sick*, is packed full of Biblical teaching, thoughtful theology, inspirational stories, and practical coaching on the mechanics and details of praying for healing, along with Next Steps sections to help you personally apply and live out what you will be learning!

ABOUT THE AUTHORS

Alex and Hannah Absalom lead Dandelion Resourcing, which empowers Christians to go and form disciple-making disciples of Jesus in naturally supernatural ways. Originally from England, they have been in church leadership since 1994, live in Long Beach CA, and with their 3 young adult sons are missionaries to the USA.

facebook.com/dandelionresourcing

twitter.com/AlexAbsalom

instagram.com/alexabsalom

Made in the USA
Las Vegas, NV
21 September 2023

77902980R00083